OXFORD WORLD'S CLASSICS

THE RECOGNITION OF ŚAKUNTALĀ

KĀLIDĀSA (*c.* fourth to fifth century CE) was the greatest poet and playwright of the classical Indian tradition. Hardly anything is known about his life, but his works suggest that he lived in northern India, possibly under the patronage of the powerful and brilliant Gupta dynasty. His surviving output consists of three (or four) long poems in Sanskrit, and three plays in a mixture of Sanskrit and Prakrit, the best-known of which is *The Recognition of Śakuntalā*, a work of unrivalled aesthetic and cultural significance. Probably based on an episode in the great Sanskrit epic, the *Mahābhārata* (*c.*500 BCE to 400 CE), *Śakuntalā* is dominated by the erotic and heroic moods characteristic of dramas of this type. The play's combination of poetry, action, plot, movement, sound, and gesture is designed to produce an ineffable experience of entrancement or aesthetic rapture in the audience. Its success in achieving this confirms its status as the supreme work of classical Indian literature.

From the time of Sir William Jones's pioneering English translation of 1789, which excited and inspired many European composers and writers (including Goethe), Kālidāsa's play has attracted considerable interest outside India, and has been translated into every major European language. It continues to be performed around the world in a variety of styles and translations.

W. J. JOHNSON was educated at the University of Sussex and Wolfson College, Oxford. He is now Senior Lecturer in Religious Studies at Cardiff University. His publications include new translations of *The Bhagavad Gita* (Oxford, 1994) and *The Sauptikaparvan of the Mahābhārata* (Oxford, 1998) for Oxford World's Classics, and *Harmless Souls* (Delhi, 1995), a study of karma and religious change in early Jainism. He is married with two sons.

OXFORD WORLD'S CLASSICS

For over 100 years Oxford World's Classics have brought readers closer to the world's great literature. Now with over 700 titles—from the 4,000-year-old myths of Mesopotamia to the twentieth century's greatest novels—the series makes available lesser-known as well as celebrated writing.

The pocket-sized hardbacks of the early years contained introductions by Virginia Woolf, T. S. Eliot, Graham Greene, and other literary figures which enriched the experience of reading. Today the series is recognized for its fine scholarship and reliability in texts that span world literature, drama and poetry, religion, philosophy and politics. Each edition includes perceptive commentary and essential background information to meet the changing needs of readers.

OXFORD WORLD'S CLASSICS

KĀLIDĀSA

The Recognition of Śakuntalā

A Play in Seven Acts

Śakuntalā in the Mahābhārata

(Mahābhārata *1.62–9*)

Translated with an Introduction and Notes by

W. J. JOHNSON

OXFORD
UNIVERSITY PRESS

OXFORD
UNIVERSITY PRESS

Great Clarendon Street, Oxford OX2 6DP

Oxford University Press is a department of the University of Oxford. It furthers the University's objective of excellence in research, scholarship, and education by publishing worldwide in

Oxford New York

Athens Auckland Bangkok Bogotá Buenos Aires Cape Town Chennai Dar es Salaam Delhi Florence Hong Kong Istanbul Karachi Kolkata Kuala Lumpur Madrid Melbourne Mexico City Mumbai Nairobi Paris São Paulo Shanghai Singapore Taipei Tokyo Toronto Warsaw

with associated companies in Berlin Ibadan

Published in the United States by Oxford University Press Inc., New York

First published as an Oxford World's Classics paperback 2001
Reissued 2008

British Library Cataloguing in Publication Data
Data available

Library of Congress Cataloging in Publication Data
Data available

ISBN 978–0–19–954060–0

23

Typeset in Ehrhardt
by RefineCatch Limited, Bungay, Suffolk

Printed and bound in Great Britain by Clays Ltd, Elcograf S.p.A.

For Pat

CONTENTS

INTRODUCTION

Kālidāsa and The Recognition of Śakuntalā

Kālidāsa is widely acknowledged as the supreme poet and playwright of the classical Sanskrit tradition, and for many, he is simply the greatest writer India has produced.[1] His surviving works consist of three long poems,[2] and three plays based on traditional themes: *Mālavikāgnimitra* (*Mālavikā and Agnimitra*), *Vikramorvaśīya* (*Urvaśī Won by Valour*), and the famous *Abhijñānaśākuntala* (*The Recognition of Śakuntalā*). He almost certainly lived in northern India, perhaps in the late fourth to the mid-fifth century CE,[3] and possibly under the patronage of the powerful and brilliant Gupta dynasty. He is likely to have belonged to the brahmin (priestly) class and, from the benedictions that open each of his plays, appears to have been a devotee of the great Hindu god Śiva, and probably of the Goddess as well;[4] but nothing is known of his life and career beyond what can be inferred from his poetry and plays. These show him to have worked in what was already an established tradition of court poetry and drama, the origins of which may have pre-dated him by a thousand years or more. However, the only surviving precursors of Kālidāsa's dramas are fragments by the Buddhist poet Aśvaghoṣa (*c.* second century CE) and, if we accept the dating given above, a number of complete plays by Bhāsa (*c.* fourth century CE).

The Recognition of Śakuntalā[5] (sometimes known as 'the Śākuntala'—i.e. 'the play about Śakuntalā'—but more popularly

[1] For the principal secondary sources for this Introduction, see the studies by Goodwin, Gerow, Miller, Gitomer, and Keith listed in the Select Bibliography.

[2] *Raghuvaṃśa* (*The Dynasty of Raghu*), *Kumārasambhava* (*The Birth of the War God*), and *Meghadūta* (*The Cloud Messenger*). *Ṛtusaṃhāra* (*The Gathering of the Seasons*) may also be genuine.

[3] We can only be certain that he lived some time between the beginning of the second century BCE and 634 CE.

[4] 'Kālidāsa' means 'servant of Kālī', a fierce form of the Goddess, who is Śiva's consort.

[5] The title of the play is not concisely translatable in a literal way, but may perhaps be rendered as: 'The Play About Śakuntalā Remembered Through the Ring of Recognition' or 'Recollection' (see Barbara Stoler Miller (ed.), *Theater of Memory: The Plays of Kālidāsa* (New York: Columbia University Press, 1984), 337, for a more detailed explanation).

simply as 'Śakuntalā', after its heroine) is generally considered to be the best of Kālidāsa's dramas and, by consensus, the paradigmatic Sanskrit play, a work of poetic brilliance and complex structure which has provided a benchmark for all classical Indian literature. Indeed, *Śakuntalā* has a cultural cachet in India similar to that associated with Shakespeare's *Hamlet* in the world at large, although it is a very different kind of play.[6] Yet to say so hardly reveals the true extent of *Śakuntalā*'s cultural significance. In the words of one commentator, it is judged by the tradition itself to be 'the validating aesthetic creation of a civilization', a play whose form and content unite to 'express persistent cultural verities'.[7]

From the time of Sir William Jones's pioneering English translation of 1789, which excited and inspired so many European composers and writers (including Goethe), Kālidāsa's play has attracted considerable interest outside India, and has been translated into every major European language. It has also been performed around the world in a variety of styles and translations. Nevertheless, *Śakuntalā* has not yet established a place in the wider western theatrical canon; for instance, it has not to date (2000) been produced by either of the national companies in Britain. No doubt, if they have considered it at all, they have thought it too remote in form and content from the experience of a European or American audience to be worth the risk. One ambition of the present translation is to inspire a revision of that critical and commercial judgement.

Kālidāsa's Play: Plot and Structure

In its broad outlines the plot of Kālidāsa's play follows an episode in the great Sanskrit epic the *Mahābhārata* (translated here as 'Śakuntalā in the *Mahābhārata*'), but with significant differences.[8] *Acts 1–3*: King Duṣyanta is hunting in the forest when he comes across an ascetic hermitage. There he meets Śakuntalā, the foster-daughter of the patriarch (Kaṇva). They fall in love and contract a

[6] If we are making a comparison with Shakespeare, *Śakuntalā* bears some surface resemblance to the late romances such as *The Winter's Tale*—a play with which an enterprising producer might fruitfully pair it.

[7] Edwin Gerow, 'Plot Structure and the Development of *Rasa* in the Śakuntalā', Pts. I and II, *Journal of the American Oriental Society*, 99: 4 (1979); 100:3 (1980), Pt. I, 564.

[8] See section on 'Kālidāsa's Sources', below, for a brief discussion of this and other possible sources.

gāndharva marriage (a secret 'love match' by mutual consent). After dispelling some troublesome demons for the ascetics, the king returns to his palace and his other wives, leaving a ring with Śakuntalā as a token of his good faith. *Act 4*: Meanwhile Śakuntalā, in love, and neglecting her duty of hospitality, inadvertently incurs the wrath of Durvāsas, a visiting ascetic. Without her knowledge he imposes a curse: she will remain unrecognized by the object of her passion until she can produce a token of recognition. In a famous scene, Śakuntalā bids farewell to her foster-father, friends, and the natural world of the forest hermitage, and, visibly pregnant with the king's child, journeys to the palace. *Act 5*: At the palace Duṣyanta fails to recognize her, and when she tries to produce the ring she discovers it has been lost on the journey. The troubled king rejects her as an impostor. Publicly humiliated, Śakuntalā is suddenly spirited away by her mother, the nymph Menakā. *Act 6*: Later, the ring (the 'recognition' of the title) is found in the belly of a fish, and taken to the king. This causes Duṣyanta to regain his memory, and he becomes filled with remorse at the rejection and loss of his wife and child. Eventually he is called back to his duty by the arrival of the god Indra's charioteer, who recruits him to lead the fight against a demon army. *Act 7*: Six years later the king is returning on an airborne chariot from his campaign against the demons. He puts down in a celestial hermitage, where he sees an extraordinary young boy playing with a lion cub. Gradually he comes to the realization that this is his son by Śakuntalā, a child called Sarvadamana (later known as Bharata) who, as foretold in Act 1, will grow up to be a world emperor. Śakuntalā herself appears; she and Duṣyanta are reunited, blessed by the gods, and prepare to return to the royal capital. The action has thus progressed from the love-permeated, natural world of Śakuntalā's forest hermitage, through the duty-bound world of the royal court, to conclude in the celestial hermitage, where love and duty are unified in a complementary relationship.

In so far as it ends where it begins, but at a higher or more integrated level, Kālidāsa's play has a sometimes obvious, sometimes more occluded spiral structure. This can be emphasized in a general way by noting what the playwright adds to the *Mahābhārata* story. The latter describes Duṣyanta on his hunting trip coming across the forest hermitage. Attempting to call on Kaṇva, he meets Śakuntalā on her own. Hearing the story of her true parentage, he persuades her to contract a *gāndharva* marriage and, after making love to her, returns to the court, promising that any son of theirs will be made heir to the kingdom. After three years' gestation a son is born to Śakuntalā. When he is a young boy, Kaṇva sends mother and son to the court, where Duṣyanta refuses to recognize them. Śakuntalā berates the king at length, instructing him in the importance of sons. Duṣyanta dismisses her, but a supernatural voice intervenes to validate Śakuntalā's story. The king formally recognizes Śakuntalā as his queen, and her son as his heir. He had only resisted because he was afraid the story of their marriage would not be believed by the people.

The crucial difference between the *Mahābhārata* version and the play is Kālidāsa's addition of a curse to explain Duṣyanta's rejection of his wife, and the related device of the ring of recognition, which eventually permits the king to regain his memory. Apart from casting the king in a morally better light, this allows the playwright to extend and effectively mirror the action from the perspective of separation and remorse in Acts 6 and 7.[9] In the process, he creates complex parallelisms, inversions, and reversals. I shall limit myself to pointing out some of the more obvious here, and refer interested readers to the secondary sources, or better still their own scrutiny of the text.[10]

The clearest way to illustrate some of the parallels and contrasts is to consider the acts as mirrored pairs (1 and 7, 2 and 6, 3 and 5).

Act 1

Duṣyanta and his charioteer arrive at a hermitage in an earthly paradise. Ascetics predict that the king will be the father of a world emperor. He discovers and is charmed by Śakuntalā.[11]

[9] There are, of course, many other differences as well: Kālidāsa's king's duty-bound destruction of local and global demons, for one.

[10] These have been been discussed by a number of commentators, although seldom with total agreement about how and where they occur. See, e.g. Edwin Gerow's articles listed in the Select Bibliography.

[11] In this, and what follows, I do not give detailed correspondences. Readers will discover these for themselves: for instance, in the first act, Duṣyanta conceals himself to watch Śakuntalā and her friends, then intervenes to remove a threat (the bee); a similar pattern of concealment and intervention takes place in relation to the child in the final act.

Act 7

Duṣyanta and a different charioteer (on loan from the god Indra), arrive at a hermitage in a celestial paradise, where the king discovers his son (exhibiting the physical signs of a world emperor) and recovers Śakuntalā. It is clear from this that the first and last acts reflect each other.[12]

Act 2

Duṣyanta, accompanied by the Vidūṣaka, is encamped in a miniature court set up in the middle of the country. Here he reflects on his encounter with Śakuntalā in Act 1 and plans her seduction in Act 3. Their separation promises to be temporary. His opportunity comes when ascetics arrive, asking him to remain there and protect them from threatening demons.

Act 6

After the discovery of his ring and the restoration of his memory, Duṣyanta, accompanied by the Vidūṣaka, appears in a pleasure garden (the country in miniature) within the court. Here he relives his first encounter with Śakuntalā through a painting. He is filled with remorse, and his separation from her seems permanent. Indra's charioteer arrives and recruits the king to protect the gods from threatening demons, thus providing him, although he does not yet know it, with the opportunity to be reunited with Śakuntalā. The 'pairing' of these two acts, as different registers of separation, is reinforced by Śakuntalā's total absence from them (she appears in each of the other five acts).

Act 3

Duṣyanta finds Śakuntalā in the countryside, discovers that his feelings are reciprocated, and suggests a *gāndharva* marriage. They suffer a temporary separation when she is called away by the senior female ascetic, Gautamī, and he is once again called to deal with some demons threatening the ascetics' rituals.

[12] This is also true of a number of characters throughout the play: for instance, the two charioteers may be paired, as may Kaṇva and Mārīca. Directors could obviously make creative use of such doublings in production.

Act 5

Śakuntalā appears to Duṣyanta in the court; she discovers that her feelings for him are apparently no longer reciprocated: he denies their marriage and disowns the child she is carrying. The king loses Śakuntalā when she is whisked away by supernatural means, starting an apparently permanent separation.

Act 4

In this pivotal and transitional act the changes are effected that allow the plot to echo itself in another register or key thereafter. Śakuntalā's marriage and pregnancy (she now carries the continuity of the religious and social order within her) necessitate her departure from the forest hermitage. Leaving behind her forest children (fawns and plants), she goes from the natural world of unfettered love to the rule- and duty-bound world of the city and the court, and to a new social status in marriage and motherhood. Thanks to the curse, of which Śakuntalā, like the king, is unaware, the promised resolution turns out to be postponed until Act 7. By that time Śakuntalā, again waiting in a hermitage, but this time a celestial one, has grown from an innocent girl into a woman with a 6-year-old child. Her second departure for the court, as Duṣyanta's recognized chief consort and the mother of his heir, is imminent as the play ends. But this time she will go in the company of her husband, a husband who was significantly absent from Act 4.

Aesthetic Theory[13] *and the Meaning of* Śakuntalā

Kālidāsa's work seems to have been more or less contemporary with the compilation of the earliest extant treatise dealing with the art of Sanskrit drama, *The Drama Manual* (*Nāṭyaśāstra*) attributed to the legendary Bharata.[14] Subsequent commentators, ancient and modern, have relied heavily on this work to analyse the elements and structure of Kālidāsa's plays, although the extent to which he follows, rather than helps to establish, the convention as presented in

[13] For a detailed description, see *Nāṭyaśāstra*, Chs. 6–7; also A. B. Keith, *The Sanskrit Drama in its Origin, Development, Theory and Practice* (Oxford: Clarendon Press, 1924; repr. Delhi: Motilal Banarsidass, 1992), *passim*, and Robert E. Goodwin, *The Playworld of Sanskrit Drama* (Delhi: Motilal Banarsidass, 1998), 177–84.

[14] Not to be confused with the Bharata who appears in the *Śakuntalā* episodes.

the treatise is by no means certain. Nevertheless, a brief outline of the aesthetic and structural considerations underlying Sanskrit drama provides a gateway to his work.[15]

In the Prologue the Actor-Manager designates *Śakuntalā* a *nāṭaka*, both a general term for drama as one of the principal forms of Sanskrit poetry or *kāvya*,[16] and a specific name for a particular kind of play, a 'heroic romance' with a royal hero. According to *The Drama Manual*,[17] all worthwhile drama has a precise purpose: the creation of a harmonious and complementary whole out of the principal emotions (*sthāyibhāva*) evoked within the play in order to engender a related, but impersonal and universalized, experience of joy and bliss in the audience. It is the particular combination of poetry, action, plot, movement, sound, and gesture that brings about this mood or *rasa*.[18] According to the theory, there is therefore nothing fortuitous about the way in which such an effect is obtained: as Robert Goodwin, drawing on T. S. Eliot, puts it, 'the aesthetic enhancement of emotion that produces *rasa* results from a subtle mix of the appropriate "objective correlatives" of the basic emotion . . . and the depiction, again via objective correlatives, of related secondary feelings'.[19] In other words, an audience of cognoscenti, educated in the subtleties of this aesthetic, have their common response conditioned, both by the specifics of the performance and by the dominant emotion or emotions that persist throughout it. Thus, a long time before postmodernism, the ancient Indians had realized that aesthetic response depends as much on the expectations and conditioning of the audience as it does on poetry, theatrical conventions, and styles of acting. Indeed, some of the later Indian commentators stressed the role of the spectator above that of the actor in achieving the aesthetic goal.[20]

Although *rasa* in itself is a single, ineffable experience of entrancement or aesthetic rapture, it is subdivided for analytical

[15] Those requiring a more detailed view of Sanskrit theatrical practices and aesthetic theory are referred to works cited in the Select Bibliography, especially translations of the *Nāṭyaśāstra* itself.

[16] Cf. Sanskrit poetry's other major form: *mahākāvya* or 'court epic'.

[17] *Nāṭyaśāstra*, chs. 6–7.

[18] Literally, 'flavour' or 'savour'.

[19] Goodwin, *The Playworld of Sanskrit Drama*, 177.

[20] See, e.g. Raniero Gnoli, *The Aesthetic Experience According to Abhinavagupta* (Varanasi: Chowkhamba Sanskrit Series, 2nd revised edn. 1968).

purposes according to the emotions, or principal feelings, that evoke it.[21] The dominant *rasa* in *Śakuntalā* is the erotic or romantic (*śṛṅgāra*) mood, corresponding to the emotion of love (*rati*). This is supported by auxiliary *rasa*, especially the *vīra* or 'heroic' mood, evoked by the emotion of energy, and closely associated with the king in his role as protector of *dharma* (the social and religious order).[22] This concentration on the unfolding of mood, through the interaction of stereotypes (king, beautiful woman, ascetic, etc.) rather than individual characters, has led some analysts to view plot, conflict, and character development as subordinate, not to say incidental, to *rasa* in the Sanskrit drama. Daniel Ingalls, for instance, chooses to stress the Sanskrit play's characterization as a *dṛśyakāvya* or 'spectacle-poem', arguing that it cannot be a 'drama' because it lacks both action and the conflict of character and principle. Mood (*rasa*) determines the play's content, as well as its form (a combination of speech, pantomime, dance, and music), and is likewise the vehicle of its plot development.[23] Less formulaic, and more consonant with the experience of the play (whether on the page or in performance), is the suggestion that, although the characters in a Sanskrit drama may be stereotypes, they nevertheless align themselves with conflicting principles,[24] in particular, the conflict or dialectic between the principles of *kāma* (pleasure or desire) and *dharma* (duty, as defined by birth and stage in life).

This may, as Miller suggests, be a 'perennial human conflict',[25] but to grasp its full significance in the Indian context, we need to know something about a classical scheme known as the four 'human goals'

[21] Theoretically enumerated as eight emotions: (1) love, (2) laughter, (3) sorrow, (4) energy, (5) anger, (6) fear, (7) disgust, and (8) amazement; which engender eight corresponding *rasa*: (1) erotic, (2) comic, (3) pathetic, (4) heroic, (5) furious, (6), fearful, (7) grotesque, and (8) wondrous.

[22] At the level of plot-structure, itself carefully analysed in *The Drama Manual* (*Nāṭyaśāstra*, ch. 21), Edwin Gerow has attempted to demonstrate in great detail how the plot of *Śakuntalā* is crucial to the realization of its aesthetic effect or *rasa*. Interested readers are referred to his 'Plot Structure and the Development of *Rasa* in the Śakuntalā', Pts. I and II.

[23] Quoted in Goodwin *The Playworld of Sanskrit Drama*, p. x. One wonders where this definition of drama leaves *Waiting For Godot*, a play in which, famously, 'nothing happens, twice'. But, of course, things do happen in *Godot*, and they happen in *Śakuntalā*; and Greek-derived models of what constitutes action, conflict, and 'drama' may not be appropriate in either case.

[24] See e.g. Goodwin, *The Playworld of Sanskrit Drama*, p. x.

[25] Miller (ed.), *Theater of Memory*, 27.

or 'pursuits' (*puruṣārtha*). These divide into three worldly pursuits—*dharma* (duty), *artha* (material success), and *kāma* (pleasure or desire)—and one whose aim is liberation from worldly existence (*mokṣa*).[26] The latter is achieved through renunciation of the other three, but especially *kāma*, which, from the orthodox renouncer's perspective, is a form of ignorance. This *puruṣārtha* scheme overlaps with another, that of *varṇāśrama-dharma*, duty according to birth and stage of life. The duties (*dharma*) of a king and a fisherman, for instance, are obviously quite different, but each attains the goal of *dharma* by following his own specific duty and not trespassing on that of others.[27] All males born into the three higher classes (*varṇa*)[28] are, however, expected, at least in theory, to progress through four stages of life (*āśrama*): student (of the *Veda*), householder, forest-dweller, and renouncer. (In so far as they fit this scheme, the male ascetics of Kaṇva's hermitage in *Śakuntalā* appear to be 'forest-dwellers'.) *Dharma* or duty is also specific to these four stages. So the prime duty of a householder is to marry and produce sons, who will feed him and his ancestors in the afterlife. Only when he has achieved that aim (the goal of *kāma*) should he retire to the forest, as a prelude, in the classical scheme, to his full renunciation of the householder's *dharma* in pursuit of *mokṣa*. The need for offspring explains the anguish of the king in Act 6 of *Śakuntalā* when he believes himself to be without an heir, and provides the main thread to Śakuntalā's argument in the *Mahābhārata* version of the story.

The king's *dharma* goes beyond this, of course: he has the primary responsibility of ensuring that conditions are right in the kingdom for the practice of all the *puruṣārthas*. This is why, in Kālidāsa's play, he is constantly being called upon to protect the ascetics and their practices from disruptive demons, the forces of

[26] By 'worldly existence' one should understand not just the present life, but the potentially endless cycle of birth, death, and rebirth, conditioned by one's actions (*karma*).

[27] As the *Bhagavad Gita* (3. 35) puts it: 'It is better to practise your own inherent duty deficiently than another's duty well. It is better to die conforming to your own duty; the duty of others invites danger': W. J. Johnson (trans.), *The Bhagavad Gita*, Oxford World's Classics (Oxford: Oxford University Press, 1994).

[28] Those of brahmin (priest), ruler or warrior, and artisan or merchant. Beneath these groups in the social hierarchy is the servant class, and lower still, although technically outside the system altogether, the 'untouchables'.

chaos and disorder that are *dharma*'s opposite (*adharma*).[29] This duty becomes extended, in the temporal space between the final two Acts, to a cosmic battle against the demons, on behalf of Indra, the king of the gods, but for the benefit of the whole world.

In return for this protection, the ascetics in *Śakuntalā* underwrite the authority (*dharma*) of the king, and through their magical powers bless his kingdom and dynasty with prosperity (*artha*).[30] Such gifts are granted by Kaṇva in the *Mahābhārata* version, and by Mārīca, Kaṇva's celestial counterpart, in the play. When things go wrong, however, when there has been dereliction of duty, the same magical power can be used *against* those responsible; and this is precisely what happens when Śakuntalā and the king are cursed by the irascible sage Durvāsas in Act 4. On a strictly ethical, rather than aesthetic reading, *dharma*—the natural order according to Brahminical values—is threatened, that is unbalanced, by the excessive nature of the king's *kāma*. This is mirrored by Śakuntalā's neglect of her duty (engendering the curse), which is also the result of single-minded *kāma*.[31] (The king, of course, is responsible for her state, and so the curse affects them both.) Balance and resolution is only attained through the birth and recognition of a son and heir (Sarvadamana/Bharata), for a 'householder' the purpose of *kāma*. This guarantees the continuity of both order (*dharma*) and prosperity (*artha*), not just for the kingdom but for the entire world: Bharata will be a *cakravartin*, a world emperor. The *Mahābhārata* version of the story is dominated by this concern, and it is increasingly stressed by Kālidāsa in the last two acts of the play. Sarvadamana's recognition as the true heir legitimizes *kāma* and reconciles it to *dharma* in both versions. In the words of Edwin Gerow, 'the conditions of love and duty (*kāma*

[29] *Dharma* here having the general sense of a social and cosmic order, barely distinguishable from the king's duty to uphold it.

[30] Such powers are generated through forms of austerity known as *tapas* (literally 'heat'). In the epics and mythological texts most ascetics seem more concerned with generating these kinds of powers than achieving liberation from rebirth (*mokṣa*).

[31] As Goodwin points out, this suspicion of *kāma* reflects the influence of asceticism and ascetic values on *dharma*, resulting in a general 'cultural ideology of self-restraint' (*The Playworld of Sanskrit Drama*, p. ix); hence the tension between ascetic influenced *dharma* and *kāma*, which have to coexist as legitimate worldly ends. *Kāma* and *mokṣa* are, of course, antithetical and exclusive: they belong to different stages of life and so do not come into direct conflict.

and *dharma*) develop from external and contingent opposites into necessary complementarities'.[32]

This reading of *The Recognition of Śakuntalā* is, as already mentioned, essentially ethical in perspective and outcome. From the aesthetic point of view, however, there can be no doubt that the play is dominated by the experience of the erotic mood, as mediated through and savoured in the experience of the ideal *rasika* or 'man of taste', that is, the king.[33] The idea, however, that there is any one cultural or aesthetic code that will 'crack' the meaning of the play is to limit its effect unnecessarily. Its ambiguities and multifaceted nature are what make it a great work of art, something it has in common with the best works of Shakespeare. Like Shakespeare, Kālidāsa has generated something of an 'industry', and *Śakuntalā*'s thematic complexities have received much critical (i.e. frequently conflicting) attention. The interested reader is directed to works cited in the Select Bibliography; here I have merely signposted some of the culturally significant themes which an educated Indian spectator of Kālidāsa's time might have been expected to recognize without reflection.

Audience and Language

It is likely that the Sanskrit dramas of Kālidāsa's time were performed by troupes of actors and dancers supported by royal patronage. Under the Guptas (*c.*350–470 CE), palaces may well have included purpose-built theatres, staffed by permanent companies

[32] Edwin Gerow, 'Sanskrit Dramatic Theory and Kālidāsa's Plays', in Miller (ed.), *Theater of Memory*, 59.

[33] See Goodwin, who points out that, according to *rasa* poetics, *kāvya* is a medium naturally aligned wiith *kāma*, so questions of duty, for instance, become questions of *feeling* about duty—a feeling whose goal is ultimately aesthetic pleasure (*The Playworld of Sanskrit Drama*, p. xv). The closeness of this aesthetic goal to the religious goal of *mokṣa* (liberation), and its capacity to rival the latter, is confirmed, perhaps, by the convergence of the two within a single system in the works of the great Kashmiri Śaivite, Abhinavagupta (*fl.* 1000 CE). On Abhinavagupta, see Gnoli, *The Aesthetic Experience According to Abhinavagupta*; Goodwin, *The Playworld of Sanskrit Drama*, ch. 1; and esp. Alexis Sanderson, 'Purity and Power Among the Brahmans of Kashmir', in M. Carrithers *et al.* (eds.), *The Category of the Person* (Cambridge: Cambridge University Press, 1985), 190–216, and 'Trika Śaivism', in M. Eliade (ed.-in-chief), *The Encyclopedia of Religions*, vol. 13 (New York: Macmillan, 1987), 15–16. On the king as ideal *rasika*, see the section on 'Verse, Prose, and the Nature of the Play', below.

under the direction of an actor-manager (see the Prologue to *Śakuntalā*). Although it was the courtly aristocracy, the princely and brahminical classes, who would have seen their world and values reflected in the plays, the audience seems, at least initially, to have been drawn from a wider social pool, ranging from the highly educated and discerning connoisseur (perhaps Kālidāsa's ideal spectator)[34] to those who had just come to enjoy the spectacle. Giving people the opportunity to watch a play was claimed by the (admittedly biased) *Drama Manual* to be an act equivalent to a religious offering, and one that brought the patron great merit.[35] Such opportunities would have been frequently provided, then as now, by the numerous religious festivals that punctuate the year, as well as by significant royal or political events.

The mixed nature of the audience is mirrored by a similar mixture in the languages employed by the playwright (Sanskrit and various types of Prakrit), and in the characters or types he depicts. By Kālidāsa's time Sanskrit had been a classical language for 800 years or more, since its codification by the grammarian Pāṇini in the fourth century BCE.[36] In other words, like Latin in medieval Europe, it had become an index of political, cultural, and religious authority, a language of scholarly and religious discourse that had to be learned by means of a special and exclusive education. Such learning was facilitated and guaranteed by the immense prestige attached to Sanskrit as the language of a collection of revealed religious texts known as the *Veda*, and it was largely controlled access to the *Veda*, via Sanskrit, that perpetuated the status accorded to the higher castes (particularly the brahmins). Under the Guptas, Sanskrit's prestige and 'refinement' led to its adoption as the preferred language of both administration and courtly literature.

The dialects most people spoke in northern India,[37] although derived from the same Vedic language as classical Sanskrit, had developed largely without codification: hence the collective noun by which the grammarians knew them, 'Prakrit', or 'natural'. These too, in time, became either religious (for the Buddhists and Jains) or

[34] The 'cognoscenti' referred to by the Actor-Manager in the Prologue (1.2). On such a 'man of taste', see below.

[35] *Nāṭyaśāstra*, 36. 80–1.

[36] One meaning of the word 'Sanskrit' is 'classified' or 'assembled'.

[37] i.e. learned as a first language, or 'mother tongue'.

literary languages, 'frozen', as it were, in the act of being memorized or written down. Meanwhile, north Indian dialects continued to change and diversify until the situation was reached that obtains in the modern world, where they are classified as separate 'languages' (Gujarati, Rajasthani, etc.). At a basic level, however, these modern languages remain mutually intelligible to many of their speakers without special learning. Something akin to this level of understanding may well have been the norm for many in the audience at the original performances of Kālidāsa's plays; that is to say, they understood little or no Sanskrit but could get by in a number of Prakrits. This understanding would have been supplemented by their reading of the third type of language employed, that of gesture.[38]

In *Śakuntalā* Sanskrit is spoken by high-caste, educated males: the king and his higher-grade officials, brahmins, and male ascetics. Females, young boys, and lower-caste men speak different kinds of Prakrit (see the List of Characters).[39] In Act 1, for instance, the king speaks Sanskrit to the three women he meets in the hermitage: they, on the other hand, reply to him, and speak to each other, in Prakrit. Conventionally, a particular kind of Prakrit was put into the mouth of a certain type of character; women, for instance, would speak one type, which was considered relatively refined, while uneducated characters would use another, considered appropriately uncouth. Similarly, one type of Prakrit would be used for prose, another for songs. As Barbara Stoler Miller has pointed out, however, Kālidāsa was not wholly bound by this convention; instead, he blended various Prakrits to exploit their dramatic effect, using them 'to complicate and enrich the verbal expressions of complex psychological states'.[40] Whether or not the dramatic Prakrits had themselves been completely stylized by Kālidāsa's time (i.e. were 'literary' constructions, distinct from the language people spoke in the streets), this usage nevertheless reflects and encompasses the social and gender hierarchy ('complementary mix') that underpins Indian society.

[38] See section on 'Staging and Stage Conventions', below.

[39] There are some exceptions, notably the comic brahmin who is the king's companion, the Vidūṣaka; in spite of his high-caste status he speaks a type of Prakrit, partly for comic effect and partly to illustrate his dubious character. Women of sufficient education (ascetics and courtesans) are occasionally permitted to speak Sanskrit. Priyaṃvadā (4.4) quotes a Sanskrit verse to her friend Anasūyā, who understands it perfectly well.

[40] Miller (ed.), *Theater of Memory*, 26.

It is these dramatic Prakrits, however, that were vulnerable to linguistic change in a way that 'frozen' Sanskrit never could be. As they were left behind by the ever-changing spoken language from which they originated, commentators supplied a Sanskrit version (a *chāyā* or 'shadow') of the Prakrits for educated readers and audiences. By the end of the ninth century Sanskrit dramas were, it seems, precisely that: performed entirely in Sanskrit. The immediate consequence of this linguistic shift was to ensure that Kālidāsa's works became entirely the preserve of a Sanskrit-speaking elite, and so equivalent, in exclusiveness of appeal, to the other genre in which he had worked, courtly poetry—a situation the playwright can hardly have anticipated.[41]

English translations cannot hope to reproduce what one scholar has called 'the aesthetically significant verbal polyphony' of the original texts.[42] Partly this is because it is impossible to gauge the degrees to which the different Prakrits were intelligible to a member (which member?) of the original audience, and so find a balance of distinct equivalents. But it is also because translating Prakrits with a patchwork of English dialects inevitably triggers irrelevant and extraneous historical and social associations, certain to distract the audience from the main concerns of the drama and persistently threatening unintended comedy.

Verse, Prose, and the Nature of the Play

A structural feature of Sanskrit drama that can survive verbal translation is the constant alternation of verse with prose. This overlaps the distinction, already mentioned, between Sanskrit and Prakrit. In fact, only nine of *Śakuntalā*'s 194 verses (in the Devanāgarī recension)[43] are in Prakrit; the rest are in variety of Sanskrit metres.[44] A

[41] The comparison with Shakespeare as, on the one hand, refined and courtly poet and, on the other, popular playwright is irresistible, although Shakespeare, of course, was only working in different idioms, not different dialects.

[42] Miller (ed.), *Theater of Memory*, 25.

[43] i.e. the one followed here. See 'Note on the Text and the Translation', below.

[44] Twenty-one different Sanskrit metres in all, plus one verse in a semi-Vedic metre in the Devanāgarī recension. For detailed descriptions of these, see M. R. Kale (ed. and trans.), *The Abhijñānaśākuntalam of Kālidāsa* with Commentary of Rāghavabhaṭṭa (Delhi: Motilal Banarsidass, repr. of 10th edn. 1994), 190–3 (of the Notes); cf. R. Pischel (ed.), *Kalidasa's Śakuntala: An Ancient Hindu Drama* (Cambridge, Mass.: Harvard

breakdown of the verses in Prakrit shows that all but one are recited or sung by eight different female characters (1.4, 3.14, 4.12, 4.16, 5.1, 5.16, 6.2, 6.3), the exception being an epigram by the low-caste Fisherman (6.1). Since they do not use Sanskrit, these are, of course, the only instances of female characters speaking verse in the entire play.

To take the Prologue and Act 1 as indicative: of the thirty-one verses spoken, twenty are given to the king, two to his driver, five to two male ascetics, three to the Actor-Manager, and one to the Actress (a Prakrit song). A similar ratio is maintained throughout the play: in the six acts in which he appears, the king speaks, on average, 64 per cent of the verse, peaking in Act 3 with 88 per cent, where he is virtually the only male character, and least active in Act 5 (36 per cent), where there are a considerable number of other male speakers. In the one act from which the king is absent (Act 4), the senior male figure (Kaṇva, in his only appearance in the play) speaks exactly 64 per cent of the verse, and so in a way becomes a substitute verse speaker for the king.

This is of more than just statistical significance: it gives us a clear insight into what kind of play we are being offered. The hero or *nāyaka* (i.e the king in *Śakuntalā*) is presented as the ideal man of 'feeling', the *rasika* or 'connoisseur' of poetry,[45] also known as the *sahṛdaya*, the ideal spectator 'whose heart is at one with the author's'.[46] The moment he feels an emotion (*bhāva*), he distils it through a poetic utterance to its corresponding *rasa* or mood, and so savours it, becoming, in a sense, the spectator of his own feeling, while at the same time involving the audience in his desire and its attendant problems. Each particular instance adds to the unfolding

University Press, Harvard Oriental Series, vol. 16, 2nd edn. 1922), 256–60, on metres in the Bengali recension. Both Sanskrit and Prakrit metres are based on prescribed patterns of heavy and light syllables. Prakrit verse, on the whole, has a more lyrical and direct effect, eschewing the metaphor and elaborated imagery of Sanskrit. When used alliteratively and with rhyme, Prakrit verse is the natural medium for song. (For more information see Miller, *Theater of Memory*, 24f.) The present translation, for reasons explained below, makes no attempt to reproduce anything but the variety of these metres in English.

[45] My argument in this section draws, builds on, and deviates from the argument in the Introduction to Goodwin's *The Playworld of Sanskrit Drama*.

[46] J. A. B. van Buitenen's translation of *sahṛdaya* in *Two Plays of Ancient India* (New York and London: Columbia University Press, 1968), 22.

of the mood of the piece as a whole for the audience to savour. As we know, the experience of this *rasa* is the principal object of the play, and the hero is the principal means by which it is activated.

Since the play is concerned to engender the erotic *rasa* in the audience, and *kāvya* is written from a male viewpoint (the king is the idealized projection of the *rasika*, the connoisseur), it is hardly surprising that women are presented primarily as the objects of the hero's desire.[47] This is another reason why female characters speak so little verse in the play (it is the connoisseur who savours and feels rapture, not the object of his attention), and why, when they do, it is often simply to provide an underscoring of the prevailing emotion, which is then integrated and savoured by a male character. Apart from the letter she composes in Act 3 (3. 14), which is immediately upstaged by the king's Sanskrit verse (3.15), Śakuntalā herself (the heroine or *nāyikā*) speaks no verse at all in the play. It is instructive to compare this with the *Mahābhārata* version of the story, where she dominates the dialogue. The epic, however, is concerned with the duties of husbands and wives in a pedagogical, not to say legalistic way, reinforcing the Brahminical status quo (Śakuntalā is orthodoxy's mouthpiece), whereas Kālidāsa's concern is to resolve the potential conflict of duty (*dharma*) and *kāma* (love) through aesthetic means (i.e. through its enactment as a means to *rasa*). (If this seems to suggest that Śakuntalā is an entirely passive figure in the play, one has only to look at Kālidāsa's distillation of her bafflement, resentment, and anger into an economic dramatic prose in Act 5 to become aware of a more complex picture.)

This aesthetic resolution is what constitutes Kālidāsa's 'peculiarity'—what distinguishes him from his sources, including the *Mahābhārata* episode.[48] Virtually every difference between the epic version of the story and Kālidāsa's play can be analysed as being at the service of *rasa* aesthetics, not least the major change in terms of the plot, the reason for Śakuntalā's rejection by the king. In the play he rejects her because his memory has been erased by Durvāsas's curse; in the epic he does so—at least, that is his eventual excuse—as a matter of *realpolitik*: the people needed the security of supernatural

[47] Noted by Goodwin, *The Playworld of Sanskrit Drama*, p. xx, n. 12.

[48] See Jonathan Bate, *The Genius Of Shakespeare* (London: Picador, 1997), ch. 5, on Shakespeare's 'peculiarity'—what he does to his sources.

validation. Apart from the requirement that the hero of the drama should be essentially blameless (this is part of the stereotypical nature of the king's character), for Kālidāsa's aesthetic to work Duṣyanta has to be *in* love, and never out of it throughout the play, even when he has forgotten who or what constitutes the object of his emotion.[49] Indeed, it is the very enjoyment of that emotion, savoured as its corresponding erotic *rasa*, which, while inadvertently causing his separation from Śakuntalā, leads directly into that other dimension of love—love-in-separation. It is this change of register that allows the erotic *rasa* to continue to be savoured until its resolution in the final-act reunion of Duṣyanta and Śakuntalā as the parents of a son and heir.

Staging and Stage Conventions

As with the Elizabethan theatre, much can be learned about the nature of Sanskrit drama by examining the conventions and techniques attached to its performance.[50] Here I confine myself to a brief indication of some of the main conventions as these might affect a reading of *Śakuntalā*, and especially of its stage directions.

Conventionally, there are four types of representation in Sanskrit drama: verbal, bodily (gesture, etc.), 'natural' or emotive,[51] and costume. As Goodwin remarks, these together 'comprise the "language" of drama as "spectacle poetry" (*dṛśyakāvya*) as opposed to verbal poetry (*śravyakāvya*)'.[52] According to *The Drama Manual*, theatres should be small enough for the audience to appreciate every nuance of the representation, including the wide repertoire of hand and facial gestures (particularly the use of the eyes).[53] These were

[49] See e.g. 5. 2.

[50] Much of the following information is taken from Keith, *The Sanskrit Drama in its Origin, Development, Theory and Practice*; David Gitomer, 'The Theater in Kālidāsa's Art', in Miller (ed.), *Theater of Memory*; and Farley Richmond, 'Suggestions for Directors of Sanskrit Plays', in Rachel van M. Baumer and James R. Brandon (eds.), *Sanskrit Drama in Performance* (Honolulu: University of Hawaii, 1981), 74–109. Along with the *Nāṭyaśāstra* itself, these provide valuable information about the conventions of Sanskrit theatre.

[51] The Eight Natural States (*sāttvika bhāvas*) are paralysis, horripilation, trembling, tears, sweat, faltering voice, loss of colour, and swoon

[52] Goodwin, *The Playworld of Sanskrit Drama*, 183, n. 8.

[53] *Nāṭyaśāstra*, 2.18–21.

considered essential to the communication of emotion and so the production of *rasa*. As Miller points out, in Act 1 of *Śakuntalā* the heroine barely speaks after encountering the king; her emotions and reactions to what is being said by Duṣyanta and her friends would have been conveyed through gesture and dance, providing a kind of visual commentary to the spoken dialogue.[54] This is evident from such, to the Western eye, alarming stage directions as, 'Śakuntalā displays all the embarrassment of erotic attraction' (p. 15). Most of the audience is likely, however, to have understood the psychological connotations and felt the emotional resonance of the gestures employed at least as easily as they would have understood the verbal language. The mimetic nature of other gestures is evident from the watering of the plants, and the attack by the bee in Act 1.

Such an emphasis on mime alerts us to the fact that performances would have been conducted on a bare stage with virtually no props. For instance, when the king makes his first entrance at the beginning of Act 1, the stage direction reads: 'Enter, on a chariot, the king, holding a bow, with an arrow in his hand, and his driver, in pursuit of a deer' (p. 7). This straightforward statement conceals the fact that the chariot, the bow and arrow, the pursuit of the deer, and the relative status of the king and charioteer would all have been represented by the particular movements and gestures of the actors. (The deer may or may not have been represented.) Flying in the air (as at the beginning of Act 7) would also have been conveyed by stylized gestures.

In addition to all this movement, entrances would have been accompanied by appropriate music, played by an on-stage ensemble, who may well have kept up a continuous musical commentary throughout the performance. The musicians were probably positioned between two doors, designed for entrances and exits, and set into a wall at the rear of the stage, behind which was a kind of green room. Curtains were sometimes drawn across the doors to permit particularly sudden entrances (see the Chamberlain's entrance on p. 73).

Unlike in the Elizabethan theatre, roles were usually played by the appropriate gender, although, as Gitomer points out, all-male and

[54] Miller, *Theater of Memory*, 18–19.

all-female troupes were known, as were transvestite parts.[55] Actors wore elaborate costumes and rich ornaments to signal their character's status, occupation, and place of origin. These distinctions would also have been apparent from the colours and shades of their makeup, and their gait.

The empty space which was the stage allowed, like Shakespeare's Globe, complete freedom with regard to location. In Act 7 of *Śakuntalā*, for instance, the action moves seamlessly from the sky to a celestial hermitage, and then to various locations within that hermitage. Such changes of locale are signalled by dialogue and movement,[56] and, for the actors or reader, by a stage direction translated as 'walking about' or 'walking around' (see, for instance, Act 4 where Kaṇva, Śakuntalā, and party wend their halting way to the boundaries of the hermitage by 'walking around' the stage). This convention is often referred to as the partitioning of the stage into zones, but that makes it sound like human chess, whereas in fact, as David Gitomer comments: 'As easily as these divisions are brought into being they may be dissolved, only to have new ones established.'[57] That is to say, they are imagined spaces, shared for the moment by actors and audience using a common convention, and as swiftly vaporized and reimagined.

Kālidāsa's Sources

A version of the story of Śakuntalā is contained in the first book of the Sanskrit epic, the *Mahābhārata* (Critical Edition, 1.62–9).[58] It has a direct bearing on the title of the epic, 'The great (*mahā*) [story] of the descendants of Bharata (*bhārata*)', since Bharata is the child born to Śakuntalā and Duṣyanta, but that is the limit of its significance for the main narrative.[59] Although it is probably not the sole source of

[55] Gitomer, 'The Theater in Kālidāsa's Art', 67.

[56] There are also various types of asides, themselves accompanied by gestures, to indicate that a character is talking to him- or herself, whispering to someone else, or speaking secretly.

[57] Gitomer, 'The Theater in Kālidāsa's Art', 74.

[58] The text of the *Mahābhārata* as we now have it was probably edited and re-edited over a period of about 900 years between *c.*500 BCE and 400 CE.

[59] Those readers who are not familiar with the *Mahābhārata*, and would like to know more about the core narrative, might begin by reading my introduction to *The Sauptikaparvan of the Mahābhārata: The Massacre at Night*, Oxford World's Classics (Oxford: Oxford University Press, 1998).

Kālidāsa's play, and may not even be its major source (although that seems to me likely), the episode is presented here both for its thematic contrasts, which bring out the peculiarity of Kālidāsa's dramatic version, and for its intrinsic literary value. In its own right the *Mahābhārata* version presents a speedy and robust treatment of a compelling story, executed in a forthright, and frequently dramatic, epic verse.[60] Above all it is poetic, but in a way quite removed from the *kāvya* of Kālidāsa, a distance which lends depth to the implied contrast. The major differences between epic and play are self-evident,[61] but some of the possible verbal echoes and thematic transpositions that may have found their way into Kālidāsa's play are indicated in the notes to the latter. (The significant ways in which Kālidāsa differs from his sources are discussed elsewhere in this Introduction.)

In addition to material taken from the *Mahābhārata* passage, Kālidāsa may have borrowed the device of the ring[62] from a Buddhist *Jātaka* story. This tells of a king who marries a girl he meets in the forest. He leaves her his signet ring, instructing her to bring it to him later, along with any male child she may have conceived. She gives birth to the Buddha-to-be (in one of his earlier lives), takes the boy to the court, but is rejected by the king, even though he secretly recognizes her. By means of a miracle the girl then forces the king to acknowledge his relation to them both.[63]

The story of Śakuntalā also appears in the *Bhāgavata Purāṇa* 9.20.8–22, where it is clearly taken from the *Mahābhārata*,

[60] I have attempted to reproduce this narrative drive by means of a fairly free translation. In its Sanskrit form the Śakuntalā episode from the *Mahābhārata*, like nearly all the rest of the epic, is in unrhymed verse. Most individual verses have thirty-two syllables each, a metre known as *śloka* or *anuṣṭubh*. Rhythm is provided by the variation of light and heavy syllables, although their pattern is not fixed throughout the whole line. Two passages (1.65.39–42 and 1.68. 27–9) are in another metre, known as *triṣṭubh*, which has forty-four syllables to the verse.

[61] For a summary, see the section on 'Kālidāsa's Play: Plot and Structure', above.

[62] But, as Kale has pointed out (*The Abhijñānaśākuntalam of Kālidāsa*, 63), rings are common enough tokens in folk-tales, as well as in life. So, one might add, are embarrassing pregnancies for the ruling classes. Apart from the ring, the whole episode looks closer to the *Mahābhārata* than to Kālidāsa's play. Perhaps a ring was involved in another version of the *Mahābhārata* story, familiar to Kālidāsa but now lost to us.

[63] E.B. Cowell, (ed.) and R. Chalmers (trans.), 'Kaṭṭhahāri-Jātaka', in *The Jātaka, or Stories of the Buddha's Former Births* (repr. Oxford: Pali Text Society, 1990), 27–9.

and in the *Padma Purāṇa* (3.1–6, Svarga Khaṇḍa).[64] The latter is a more elaborate version which, according to most analysts, combines elements from Kālidāsa with the epic version. Given the uncertainties of dating material in the *Purāṇas* (not to mention Kālidāsa himself), it is possible, however, that it is the playwright who draws on the *Padma Purāṇa*, rather than vice versa. But none of this detracts from Kālidāsa's power to make his sources wholly his own.

[64] Reproduced in Sanskrit in Kale, *The Abhijñānaśākuntalam of Kālidāsa*, 102–9.

NOTE ON THE TEXT AND THE TRANSLATION

Early in the process of translation I decided that I should be selling both Kālidāsa and a modern non-Sanskrit reading audience short if this were not first and foremost a performing (i.e. performable) version of the play. The works of Kālidāsa, like those of any other great playwright, only come fully alive on stage: the words on the page are the beginning of the process, not its culmination. This is even more the case when they have been translated into another language. The fact that Kālidāsa was also a great poet should not seduce us into treating his plays as simply anthologies of poetry. To some extent this *has* been his fate in India, as much as it has been Shakespeare's in the West; but while the latter is frequently enough performed, and his theatrical context well enough known to redress the balance, Kālidāsa needs more assistance once he is uprooted from his home culture.

Comparing the two major recensions of the text of *Śakuntalā*, I therefore came to the conclusion that, in the modern theatre, and in translation, the Devanāgarī recension would work better than the Bengali.[1] I do not claim that the former is Kālidāsa's orginal version, or that it necessarily worked better in the Sanskrit theatre; others have argued the merits of both versions.[2] The major difference between the two recensions is the presence of twenty-seven additional

[1] My translation is based on the tenth edition of M. R. Kale's text of the Devanāgarī recension, *The Abhijñānaśākuntalam of Kālidāsa* (conveniently still in print—although prone to misprints—and available to students in India and the West), a text established by the earliest known author of a complete commentary on the play, Rāghavabhaṭṭa (in the late fifteenth century). (Kale's edition includes Rāghavabhaṭṭa's commentary in Sanskrit.) I compared this throughout with Pischel's edition of the Bengali recension (*Kalidasa's Śakuntala: An Ancient Hindu Drama*), but resisted the temptation to produce a composite version. Since my translation is not rigidly literal there seemed little point in discussing variant readings in the notes for the bafflement of readers who have no Sanskrit, especially since such variants involve, for the most part, questions of nuance rather than radical differences of meaning. My own understanding of the text was helped immeasurably both by Kale's notes and by Miller's translation of the Devanāgarī version in *Theater of Memory*.

[2] For contrasting views, see, e.g. Chandra Rajan, *Kālidāsa: The Loom of Time*, 13–16; and Miller (ed.), *Theater of Memory*, 333–5; cf. Dileep Kumar Kanjilal (ed.), *A Reconstruction of the Abhijñānaśākuntalam* (Calcutta: Calcutta Sanskrit College, 1980).

verses in the Bengali version (notably in Act 3, where they prolong the dialogue between the king and Śakuntalā), and some extra prose passages. There is no doubt that the extra verses expand the erotic mood, but they perhaps add nothing to it in terms of effect. Dramatically they bring the play to a halt, and may well, as Miller has suggested, have been added at a patron's request (they may not even be by Kālidāsa himself).[3] The extra prose usually adds little but explicitness. In the wake of Beckett and Pinter, where less means more, a contemporary Western audience would hardly seem to need such assistance.[4]

Discussion of how a play might have been performed in Kālidāsa's time has, of course, a historical interest; but if the play itself is to survive as living theatre, then it has to be rediscovered in new circumstances, with new forms and new techniques. Attempts to reproduce the forms of Sanskrit theatre, or indeed Sanskrit verse, in other cultural circumstances and different languages are little better than exotic autopsies, dissections of the picturesque but immobile dead. Such autopsies have their own fascination, but if *Śakuntalā* cannot come alive for a modern, non-Sanskritic audience, the play remains in the the dissecting-room, from which it is only a short journey back to the morgue.

This is precisely where translations that strive for a tone and rhythm in the new language which is entirely their own, yet at the same time true to the elusive spirit of the original, can help to save such works from oblivion. (Notable successes with the translation and production of classical Greek drama in the modern world might show Sanskritists the way.) Though some might think it blasphemy to say so, great works—and especially great works from distant cultures and remote pasts—can be liberated as much as diminished by translation. Indeed, shrinkage is a price worth paying to achieve liberation from forms that are no longer meaningful, and the chance to remake the original as something new. Those who say that Kālidāsa's poetry is untranslatable might as well make a bonfire of his works as far as most of the world is concerned. What use is it to tell the reader about the wonderful but untranslatable nature of *kāvya*, when hardly any will, or can, take the trouble to learn the Sanskrit

[3] See Miller (ed.), *Theater of Memory*, 334–5.

[4] Those who do want more are referred to the translations by Coulson and Rajan listed in the Select Bibliography.

needed to decide for themselves? This is to be faithful to the poet, after a fashion, but to abandon, and so betray his work.

To remain—indeed, to become—a '*world's* classic', a play needs to be tested and reformed in translation and performance by each generation. What Peter Brook has written about the absurdity of trying to 'perform the play as Shakespeare wrote it', applies with equal force to the works of Kālidāsa: 'All that one knows is that he wrote a chain of words that have in them the possibility of giving birth to forms that are constantly renewed. There is no limit to the virtual forms that are present in a great text. A mediocre text may only give birth to a few forms, whereas a great text, a great piece of music, a great opera score are true knots of energy.'[5] This translation is offered as simply another such form, born from the chain of words that Kālidāsa, in the characterization of his Actor-Manager, 'strung together'. My aim, therefore, has been to convey across cultures and time, and without exoticism, some of the poetic and emotional truth latent in this play. To that end I have searched, however inadequately, for language that might produce for a modern Western audience an aesthetic effect similar or equivalent to the charge and resonance of the original. In doing so my perspective has, paradoxically, converged with that of the Sanskrit aestheticians who, in their quest for a universal and transcendent *rasa*, assumed the basic unity of human emotional and metaphysical experience. The degree to which *Śakuntalā* has meaning for us now depends, therefore, upon the degree to which we can recognize ourselves in and through Kālidāsa's transformative art.

My thanks go to Gareth John, Sophia Kanaouti, Roshan Kissoon, Emma Salter, and Girija Shettar, who confirmed my view that Kālidāsa's play works best on stage. Thanks are also due to the Department of Religious and Theological Studies, Cardiff University, and the University of Wales Conference Centre at Gregynog, who provided the space for us to try out parts of this translation in performance. I am also grateful to Dr Rupert Gethin for supplying me with copies of some secondary sources.

[5] Peter Brook, *There Are No Secrets* (Methuen: Methuen Drama, 1993), 52–3.

SELECT BIBLIOGRAPHY

This is not intended to be an exhaustive or authoritative bibliography for the study of classical Indian drama. The works listed here are those I have consulted and found useful for my translation, Introduction, and notes. Many have extensive bibliographies in their own right, and the reader wishing to venture further into this field will need to consult them. As will be evident from their titles, a number of general and introductory works on Indian culture and Hinduism have also been included.

Texts and Translations

Abhijñānaśākuntalam

Coulson, Michael (trans.), *Three Sanskrit Plays* (Harmondsworth: Penguin Books, 1981). Includes '*Śakuntalā* by Kālidāsa', a translation of Pischel's edition of the Bengali recension, and translations of '*Rākshasa's Ring* by Viśākhadatta', and '*Mālatī and Mādhava* by Bhavabhūti'.

Emeneau, M. B. (trans.), *Kālidāsa's Abhijñana-Śakuntala* (California: University of California Press, Berkeley and Los Angeles, 1962). Translated from the Bengali recension.

Jones, Sir William (trans.), *Sacontalá, or, The Fatal Ring: An Indian Drama by Cálidás* (Calcutta: Joseph Cooper, 1789); repr. of 1799 edn. in Michael J. Franklin (ed.), *Sir William Jones: Selected Poetical and Prose Works* (Cardiff: University of Wales Press, 1995), 213–97.

Kale, M. R. (ed. and trans.), *The Abhijñānaśākuntalam of Kālidāsa* with Commentary of Rāghavabhaṭṭa (Delhi: Motilal Banarsidass, repr. of 10th edn., 1994). The edition of the Devanāgarī recension used as the basis for this translation.

Kanjilal, Dileep Kumar (ed.), *A Reconstruction of the Abhijñānaśākuntalam* (Calcutta: Calcutta Sanskrit College, 1980). Essentially an edition of the Bengali recension.

Miller, Barbara Stoler (ed.), *Theater of Memory: The Plays of Kālidāsa* (New York: Columbia University Press, 1984). This includes *Śakuntalā and the Ring of Recollection*, a translation by Miller of the Devanāgarī recension, and translations of Kālidāsa's two other plays, *Urvasī Won By Valor* (trans. David Gitomer) and *Mālavikā and Agnimitra* (trans. Edwin Gerow).

Pischel, R. (ed.), *Kalidasa's Śakuntala: An Ancient Hindu Drama* (Cambridge, Mass.: Harvard University Press, Harvard Oriental Series, vol. 16, 2nd edn. 1922). The standard academic edition of the Bengali recension.

Radice, William (ed. with intro.), *Śakuntalā* by Kālidāsa, trans. Michael Coulson; with 'The Story of Śakuntalā from the *Mahābhārata*', trans. Peter Khoroche; *Śakuntalā*, by Abanindranath Tagore, trans. William Radice; '*Śakuntalā*: A Tale Retold in Pahari Miniatures', by Daljeet Khare (London: The Folio Society, 1992). Coulson's translation is a reprint from *Three Sanskrit Plays* (see above).

Rajan, Chandra (trans.), *Kālidāsa: The Loom of Time: A Selection of His Plays and Poems* (New Delhi: Penguin Books (India), 1990). Includes *Abhijñānaśākuntalam* (*The Recognition of Śakuntalā*), a translation of Kanjilal's edition, as well as translations of two of Kālidāsa's poems: *Ṛtusamhāram* and *Meghadūtam*.

Mahābhārata

Ganguli, Kisari Mohan (trans.) [early edns. ascribed to the publisher, P. C. Roy], *The Mahabharata of Krishna-Dwaipayana Vyasa*, 12 vols. (1884–99; 2nd edn. Calcutta, 1970; repr. New Delhi: Munshiram Manoharlal, 1970; 5th edn. 1990), vol. 1: *Ādi Parva*. This is a complete translation of the vulgate text, not that of the Critical Edition, which it pre-dates.

Mahābhāratam with the commentary of Nīlakaṇṭha, *Ādiparva* (Poona: Chitrashala Press, 1929)

Peter Khoroche (trans.), 'The Story of Śakuntalā from the *Mahābhārata*', in William Radice (ed. with intro.), *Śakuntalā* by Kālidāsa (London: Folio Society, 1992). This is apparently a translation of the vulgate.

Sukthankar, Vishnu S., Belvalkar, S. K., Vaidya, P. L., *et al.*, eds. *Mahābhārata* (Critical Edition), 19 vols. plus 6 vols. of indexes (Poona: Bhandarkar Oriental Research Institute, 1933–72), vol 1: *Ādi Parvan*. The edition used as the basis of this translation of the Śakuntalā episode.

van Buitenen, J. A. B. (trans. and ed.), *The Mahābhārata 1: The Book of the Beginning* (Chicago and London: University of Chicago Press, 1973). This is a translation of Book 1 (*Ādiparva*) of the Critical Edition, with introductory material and notes.

Nāṭyaśāstra

Ghosh, Manomohan (ed. and trans.), *The Nāṭyaśāstra, Ascribed to Bharata-Muni*, vol. 1 (chs. 1–27) (2nd rev. edn. Calcutta: Manisha Granthalaya, 1967); vol. 2 (chs. 28–36) (Calcutta: The Asiatic Society, 1961).

Rangacharya, Adya (trans.), *The Nāṭyaśāstra* (rev. edn. New Delhi: Munshiram Manoharlal, 1996).

Other Works

Basham, A. L., *The Wonder That Was India* (New York: Grove Press, 1959).

Bate, Jonathan, *The Genius Of Shakespeare* (London: Picador, 1997).

Baumer, Rachel van M., and Brandon, James R. (eds.), *Sanskrit Drama in Performance* (Honolulu: University of Hawaii, 1981).

Brandon, James R. (ed.), *The Cambridge Guide to Asian Theatre* (Cambridge: Cambridge University Press, 1993).

Brockington, J. L., *The Sanskrit Epics* (Leiden: Brill, 1998).

Brook, Peter, *There Are No Secrets* (Methuen: Methuen Drama, 1993).

Brown, John Russell, *New Sites for Shakespeare: Theatre, The Audience and Asia* (London and New York: Routledge, 1999).

Byrski, M. Christopher, 'Sanskrit Drama as an Aggregate of Model Situations', in Baumer and Brandon (eds.), *Sanskrit Drama in Performance*, 114–66.

Coulson, Michael, *Sanskrit: An Introduction to the Classical Language* (New York: Teach Yourself Books, Hodder & Stoughton, 1st pub. 1976; numerous reprints).

Cowell, E. B. (ed.) and Chalmers, R. (trans.), 'Kaṭṭhahāri-Jātaka', in *The Jātaka, or Stories of the Buddha's Former Births* (repr. Oxford: Pali Text Society, 1990).

Doniger, Wendy, with Smith, Brian K. (trans.), *The Laws of Manu* (Harmondsworth: Penguin Books, 1991).

Figueira, Dorothy Matilda, *Translating the Orient: The Reception of Śākuntala in Nineteenth-Century Europe* (New York: State University of New York Press, Albany, 1991).

Franklin, Michael J. (ed.), *Sir William Jones: Selected Poetical and Prose Works* (Cardiff: University of Wales Press, 1995).

Gerow, Edwin, 'Plot Structure and the Development of *Rasa* in the Śakuntalā', Pts. I and II, *Journal of the American Oriental Society*, 99:4 (1979), 559–72; 100:3 (1980), 267–82.

—— '*Rasa* as a Category of Literary Criticism', in Baumer and Brandon (eds.), *Sanskrit Drama in Performance*, 226–57.

—— 'Sanskrit Dramatic Theory and Kālidāsa's Plays', in Miller (ed.), *Theater of Memory: The Plays of Kālidāsa*.

Gitomer, David, 'The Theater in Kālidāsa's Art', in Miller (ed.), *Theater of Memory: The Plays of Kālidāsa*.

Gnoli, Raniero, *The Aesthetic Experience According to Abhinavagupta* (Varanasi: Chowkhamba Sanskrit Series, 2nd revised edn. 1968).

Goodwin, Robert E., *The Playworld of Sanskrit Drama* (Delhi: Motilal Banarsidass, 1998).

Hardy, F., *The Religious Culture of India: Power, Love and Wisdom* (Cambridge: Cambridge University Press, 1994).

Insler, Stanley, 'The Shattered Head Split and the Epic Tale of Śakuntalā', *Bulletin d'Études Indiennes*, 7–8 (1989–90), 97–139.

Jamison, Stephanie W., *Sacrificed Wife/Sacrificer's Wife: Women, Ritual, and Hospitality in Ancient India* (New York: Oxford University Press, 1996).

Keith, Arthur Berriedale, *The Sanskrit Drama in its Origin, Development, Theory and Practice* (1st pub. Oxford: Clarendon Press, 1924; repr. Delhi: Motilal Banarsidass, 1992).

Kramrisch, Stella, *The Presence of Śiva* (Princeton: Princeton University Press, 1981).

Miller, Barbara Stoler, 'Kālidāsa's World and his Plays', in B. S. Miller (ed.), *Theater of Memory: The Plays of Kālidāsa* (New York: Columbia University Press, 1984).

O'Flaherty, Wendy Doniger, *Hindu Myths: A Sourcebook Translated from the Sanskrit* (Harmondsworth: Penguin Books, 1st pub. 1975; repr. 1980).

Raghavan, V., 'Sanskrit Drama in Performance', in Baumer and Brandon (eds.), *Sanskrit Drama in Performance*, 9–44.

Richmond, Farley, 'Suggestions for Directors of Sanskrit Plays', in Baumer and Brandon (eds.), *Sanskrit Drama in Performance*, 74–109.

—— Swann, Darius L., and Zarrilli, Phillip B. (eds.), *Indian Theatre: Tradition of Performance* (Honolulu: University of Hawaii, 1990).

Sanderson, Alexis, 'Purity and Power among the Brahmans of Kashmir', in M. Carrithers *et al.* (eds.) *The Category of the Person* (Cambridge: Cambridge University Press, 1985), 190–216.

—— 'Trika Śaivism', in M. Eliade (ed.-in-chief), *The Encyclopedia of Religions*, vol. 13 (New York: Macmillan, 1987), 15–16.

Stutley, Margaret, and Stutley, James, *A Dictionary of Hinduism* (London: Routledge & Kegan Paul, 1977).

van Buitenen, J. A. B. (trans.), *Two Plays of Ancient India* (New York and London: Columbia University Press, 1968). Contains 'The Little Clay Cart' by Śūdraka and 'The Minister's Seal' by Viśākhadatta.

Further Reading in Oxford World's Classics

Bhagavad Gita, trans. and ed. W. J. Johnson.
The Pañcatantra, trans. and ed. Patrick Olivelle.
The Sauptikaparvan of the Mahābhārata, trans. W. J. Johnson.

NOTE ON THE PRONUNCIATION OF SANSKRIT WORDS

The following may act as an approximate guide, but for detailed information on the pronunciation of Sanskrit the reader should consult a work such as Michael Coulson's *Sanskrit: An Introduction to the Classical Language*. In the Introduction and Explanatory Notes some terms have been anglicized: 'brahmin' for *brāhman* (a priest), and so 'Brahminical' instead of 'Brahmanical', and so on.

Sanskrit	as in *English*
a	c*u*t
ā	f*a*r
i	s*i*t
ī	m*e*
u	p*u*t
ū	t*oo*
ṛ	*ri*sk
e	pr*ay*
ai	s*i*gh
o	h*o*pe
au	s*ou*nd
c	*ch*urch
v	close to the English *w*
ś	*sh*ame
ṣ	di*sh*
ḥ	as in English but with a faint echo of the preceding vowel
ṭ etc.	as in English, but with the tongue further back in the mouth
ṅ, ṇ	have a nasal quality
ñ,	ca*ny*on
kh, gh, ch, jh, ṭh, ḍh, th, dh, ph, bh	aspirated—as in 'ho*th*ouse', (*not* 'wi*th*'), 'she*ph*erd', clu*bh*ouse', etc.
ṃ	nasalizes the preceding vowel sound, as in French *bon*

THE RECOGNITION OF ŚAKUNTALĀ

A Play in Seven Acts

THE CHARACTERS OF THE PLAY

IN ORDER OF APPEARANCE

S = Sanskrit speaker; P = Prakrit speaker

Actor-Manager (S)	manager and director of the company; may play the hero
Actress (P)	wife of the Actor-Manager; plays the heroine
Driver (S)	the king's charioteer and companion
King Duṣyanta (S)	the hero (*nāyaka*); king of the lunar dynasty of Puru
Vaikhānasa (S)	a more solitary type of forest-dwelling ascetic; follower of Kaṇva
Two Ascetics (S)	pupils of Kaṇva
Śakuntalā (P)	the heroine (*nāyikā*); daughter of the royal sage Viśvāmitra and the nymph Menakā; foster-daughter of the ascetic Kaṇva
Anasūyā (P)	young female ascetic; friend of Śakuntalā; her name means 'without envy'
Priyaṃvadā (P)	young female ascetic; friend of Śakuntalā; her name means 'sweet talker'
Ascetic (off-stage) (S)	follower of Kaṇva
Vidūṣaka (Mādhavya) (P)	overweight brahmin; friend and confidant of the king
Attendants (P)	the king's female bow-bearers/bodyguards
Doorkeeper (Raivataka) (P)	
General (S)	commander of the king's army
Two Seers (S)	young ascetics in Kaṇva's hermitage
Karabhaka (P)	royal messenger
Assistant Sacrificer (S)	follower of Kaṇva
Gautamī (P)	senior female ascetic
Voice in the Air (Act 3) (S)	
Durvāsas (off-stage) (S)	powerful and irascible ascetic

Pupil (Viṣkambhaka) (S)	pupil of Kaṇva
Ascetic (off-stage) (S)	follower of Kaṇva
Three Hermit Women (P)	female ascetics in Kaṇva's hermitage
First Young Ascetic (Nārada) (S)	follower of Kaṇva
Second Young Ascetic (S)	follower of Kaṇva
Kaṇva (S)	brahmin sage; head of the forest hermitage; Śakuntalā's foster-father; also known as Kāśyapa
Śārṅgarava (S)	ascetic; follower of Kaṇva
Voice in the Air (Act 4) (S)	
Voice (Haṃsapadikā) (P)	one of Duṣyanta's consorts
Chamberlain (Vātāyana) (S)	chief officer of the royal household
Doorkeeper (Vetravatī) (P)	female attendant.
Two Bards (off-stage) (S)	
Śāradvata (S)	ascetic; follower of Kaṇva
Court Priest (Preceptor Somarāta) (S)	
Two Policemen (P)	
Chief of Police (Mitrāvasu) (P)	the king's brother-in-law
Man (P)	a fisherman
Sānumatī (P)	a nymph; friend of Śakuntalā's mother Menakā
First Gardener (Parabhṛtikā—'Little Cuckoo') (P)	
Second Gardener (Madhukarikā—'Little Bee') (P)	
Caturikā (P)	maidservant.
Bowbearer (P)	female attendant
Mātali (S)	charioteer of Indra, king of the gods
Boy (Sarvadamana) (P)	son of Śakuntalā and Duṣyanta; afterwards known as Bharata
Two Female Ascetics (P)	
Mārīca (S)	divine sage; head of the celestial hermitage; father of Indra, king of the gods
Aditi (P)	Mārīca's wife.
Pupil (Gālava) (S)	pupil of Mārīca

Because of the structure of the play (see the Introduction), many of these characters could be creatively doubled (played by the same actors) in production, for example, the two charioteers; Kaṇva and Mārīca; Gautamī and Aditi; and others.

PROLOGUE

*Benediction.**

prayer

Through the Creator's first creation—water, (1)
Through the ritual oblations's transport—fire,
Through the chanting priest—the reciter,
Through those twin chronometers—moon and solar fire,
Through the echoing vault of reverberating ether,
Through primal matter—Earth—all-seeding mother,
Through pure air, breath of the living breather,
Through these eight palpable embodiments of the great Lord Śiva,*
May the great Lord Himself be your protector.

[*After the benediction*

ACTOR-MANAGER [*looking towards the curtain**]. Angel, if you've finished making-up, come and join me out here.

ACTRESS [*entering*]. Here I am, darling.

ACTOR-MANAGER. Dearest, we've got a highbrow—well, a mostly highbrow audience in tonight, and we're giving them a romance with a new plot, strung together by Kālidāsa—*The Recognition of Śakuntalā*. So the actors need to be on top form.

ACTRESS. Don't worry, darling. You've rehearsed the piece so well, we'll be word perfect, and the audience will be all ears and eyes.

ACTOR-MANAGER. I'll tell you the truth, angel:

It's only when the cognoscenti applaud— (2)
And only then—a director can afford
To believe he's master of his craft.
Even the most devout
And highly trained practitioners
Feel self-doubt.

ACTRESS. That's so true, darling. Now, tell me, dear, what was it you wanted me to do?

ACTOR-MANAGER. What else but put the audience in the mood

with a soothing song. So sing about the summer that's just begun—the season made for pleasure—for now:

As the dusty body floats in the cooling stream, (3)
The days are changed by dusk to strange delight—
Days of easy sleep in wooded depths,
Days stirred and drugged by scented breeze—
The breathing forest
Fragrant with bignonia leaves.

ACTRESS. If that's what you'd like. [*She sings*

The mimosa has a blossom—delicate, exquisite— (4)
A stamen gently brushed by black woodland bees.
And lovely youthful women—so delicate, exquisite—
Wear its blossoms in their ears
Where they tremble in the breeze.

ACTOR-MANAGER. Beautifully sung, darling! As though in a painting, the entire audience has had their emotion coloured by your melody. So, now—what shall we perform to sustain the mood?

ACTRESS. If you don't mind me saying so, dearest, haven't you already announced that *Śakuntalā* is the play to be performed?

ACTOR-MANAGER. What would I do without you, darling! Just for a moment I'd completely forgotten that. But only because:

Your captivating, full-impassioned song (5)
Ravished me with force, and carried me away—*
Just as the headlong rush of a spotted deer
Carries this king, Duṣyanta,* into our play.

[*Exit* ACTOR-MANAGER *and* ACTRESS

ACT 1

Enter, on a chariot, the KING, *holding a bow, with an arrow in his hand, and his* DRIVER, *in pursuit of a deer.*

DRIVER [*glancing from the king to the deer*]. Ageless Lord!

Glancing from that black-buck to you, bow drawn, (6)
I see Śiva himself, in human form,
Pursuing the chase.*

KING. Driver, that deer has drawn us far enough. Even now:

He ever turns to see our chariot in pursuit (7)
Arching his tender neck, his body like a blade
Bent point to scabbard to evade
My homing shaft.
From his mouth, fatigue agape,
Foam-flecked, half-chewed,
Darbha grass* has strewed
His wake.
See! There he is—so great his soaring bound
He travels more by air than lumpen ground.

[*In sudden bewilderment*] But why now can I barely see him, though I was in close pursuit?

DRIVER. My Lord, the ground was uneven, so I drew in the reins and slackened the chariot's speed. But now we're on the flat again, he'll not be difficult to catch.

KING. Then release the reins.

DRIVER. As you command my king. [*Miming the increased speed of the chariot*] Look, look, my lord!

Their reins relaxed, these horses start to race, (8)
Frustration at the deer's speed whips up their pace,
Their ears are pricked, their plumes no longer shake,
Their bodies thrust the air apart, their wake

Is thunder; in our tracks they leave for dust
The very dust they raised . . .

KING. It's true—better than the horses of the sun, or Indra's steeds,*
our stallions surge ahead.

What seemed minute, suddenly fills my sight,   (9)
And broken halves and fragments now unite.
The skewed ways of nature are, through the eye,
Made straight—nothing is far from me or nigh,
So swiftly does this chariot take its flight.

Driver—watch it die!

Why'd they go running if we can't kill?.

[He takes aim with an arrow

A VOICE OFF-STAGE. King! Don't shoot! Don't kill him! This deer
belongs to the hermitage!

DRIVER [hearing the voice and looking around]. My lord, some
ascetics have planted themselves between the black-buck and you,
right in the flight-path of your arrow.

KING [urgently]. Then rein in the horses!

DRIVER. At once.   [He brings the chariot to a halt

Enter VAIKHĀNASA with TWO ASCETICS (his pupils).

VAIKHĀNASA [holding up his hand]. King, this is a hermitage deer.
You should not—you must not kill it!

Indeed, indeed, no missile should be shot,   (10)
Scorching, like a flame through velvet petals,
This young fawn's tender head.
Alas, what is the filigree life
In this poor animal's frame,
Beside the adamantine rain
Of bowshot?

Drop your deadly arrow's aim—yours is an arm   (11)
To defend the oppressed, not do them harm.

KING. It is withdrawn.   [He is as good as his word

VAIKHĀNASA. This is worthy of the light of Puru's race.*

Great Lord of the Lunar Dynasty,* (12)
May you have a son
With all your virtues,
Destined to rule the world.*

TWO ASCETICS [*raising their forearms in salutation*]. Yes! May you have a son destined to rule the world.

KING [*with a bow*]. The blessings of a brahmin are always accepted.

VAIKHĀNASA. Great king, we were on our way to collect wood for the sacrificial fire. There, on the banks of the Mālinī river, is the venerable Kaṇva's hermitage. If it isn't a distraction, go in, and receive the hospitality due to a guest. And

Once you've seen the beautiful rites the ascetics perform, (13)
Free of all disruption,
You'll realize, then, how far your own bow-scarified arm,
Reaches to give protection.

KING. Is the sage now at home?

VAIKHĀNASA. Not long ago he left his daughter Śakuntalā to look after his guests, and went himself to Somatīrtha to appease the gods on her behalf, and avert her hostile fate.*

KING. Well then! I'll see her instead. No doubt she'll tell the great sage how I've made my devotions.

VAIKHĀNASA. We'll go on now.

[*Exit* VAIKHĀNASA *and the* TWO ASCETICS

KING. Driver, whip up the horses! Let's purify ourselves with the sight of this holy hermitage.

DRIVER. As your lordship commands.

[*He mimes the movement of the chariot again*

KING [*looking around*]. Even if we hadn't been told, it would be obvious we're on the outskirts of the hermitage's ascetic-groves.

DRIVER. How?

KING. Don't you see, my friend? Here

Beneath the trees lie grains of wild rice, slipped (14)
From lips of hollow trunks, where parrots nest;
A scattering of oily stones betrays
The pounding of iṅgudi nuts;* at graze,
The confident deer stroll by undistressed,
And tolerate our noise; here, water has dripped
From the fringes of bark garments* to make
New paths from the river, or from some lake.

The roots of these trees are washed continuously (14a)
By the breeze-rippled waters of dug canals;
The drifting smoke of sacrificial *ghee**
Matts the white lustre of fresh young shoots; small
Deer crop the new darbha crop,
Fearlessly and slow,
From dappled shadow
To dappled shadow,
To deeper shadows still.

DRIVER. It's all as you say.

KING [*going a little further*]. We mustn't disturb the inhabitants of the ascetic's grove. Stop the chariot, and I'll get down here.

DRIVER. I'm reining in . . . You can dismount now, my lord.

KING [*stepping down*]. Driver, all men should look modest and humble when they enter such a holy grove—so take these. [*He hands his driver his insignia and bow*] And while I'm with these hermits, you'll have time to wash the horses down.

DRIVER. As you command, sire.

[*Exit* DRIVER

KING [*turning and seeing*]. Here's the entrance to the hermitage. I'll go in.

[*As he enters, it is apparent from his gesture that some omen has struck him*

So still a place, yet now this vein throbs in my arm, (15)
Presaging some woman's charm.*

In an ashram? Destiny
Is fixed, and all doors open onto what must be.

A VOICE OFF-STAGE. This way, my friends, this way.

KING [*listening*]. Ah, voices from south of that grove. I'll go in that direction. [*Turning and looking*] Yes! Those hermitage girls are coming this way to water the young trees, each balancing a jug that seems made for her alone. [*With intensity*] Oh, but they make a charming sight!

If such beauty thrives in the realm of trees— (16)
Beauty rare in courtesans' private rooms—
Wild creepers have qualities that, with ease,
Surpass our cultivated garden blooms.

In the depths of this shadow, I'll wait for them now.

[*Stands, watching them*

Enter ŚAKUNTALĀ, *occupied as described, with two female friends,* ANASŪYĀ *and* PRIYAṂVADĀ.

ŚAKUNTALĀ. Over here, my friends, over here!

ANASŪYĀ. Dear Śakuntalā, I suspect father Kaṇva loves the ashram's trees even more than he loves you—for, delicate as jasmine blossom yourself, he has still appointed you to water their roots.

ŚAKUNTALĀ. It's not just father's instructions. I love them like sisters.

[*Mimes watering the trees*

KING. What's this? She's Kaṇva's daughter? Then it hardly seems right that the holy sage should have assigned her the menial tasks of the ashram.

Indeed, the seer, who would put to duty (17)
And penance this supreme natural beauty,
Tries to shape mahogany or metal
With the rim of a dark lotus petal.

Let it be. I'll step aside and watch her discreetly. [*He does so*

ŚAKUNTALĀ. Friend, Anasūyā, I can hardly breathe in this bark blouse—Priyaṃvadā has pulled it far too tight. Just loosen it a little, will you?

ANASŪYĀ. There you are. [*Loosens it*

PRIYAṂVADĀ [*laughing*]. It's nothing to do with me! Scold your own youth that makes your breasts swell so.

KING. She's right:

Tied to her shoulder by a makeshift knot, (17a)
The mottled garment chafes her youthful breasts,
And folds her, like a blossom in a pale bud.

That bark dress certainly doesn't reveal her figure, yet somehow her beauty is enhanced—jewellery couldn't do it better. Indeed:

The lotus glows, though weeds drag down its roots, (18)
A dark penumbra makes the moon more light,
And this slight child beggars her beggar's clothes—
All rags are gowns on girls who burn this bright.

ŚAKUNTALĀ [*looking in front of her*]. Look how this mango seems to beckon, how its shoots implore me in the breeze. I must water it.

[*She circumambulates it*

PRIYAṂVADĀ. Dear Śakuntalā, stay there just for a moment . . . With you next to it, that tree looks as though it's been married to a beautiful, sinuous vine.

ŚAKUNTALĀ. 'Priyaṃvadā's' the right name for you—'sweet talker',* indeed!

KING. Sweet, but true, are Priyaṃvadā's words. For

Her lower lip's as red as a fresh young bud, (19)
Her arms are tender shoots, supple yet trim,
And like a longed-for blossom, gathering strength,
Youth pushes up through all her limbs.

ANASŪYĀ. Dear Śakuntalā, here's that jasmine you call Light of the Forest. She's chosen the fragrant mango as her bridegroom.* You've forgotten her.

ŚAKUNTALĀ. Only when I forget myself. [*Approaches the jasmine and gazes at it*] My dear friend, the union of this tree and this jasmine has taken place at the most wonderful time—the jasmine is a young plant, covered in fresh blossoms, the mango has soft buds, and is ready for enjoyment . . .

[*She stands gazing at them*

PRIYAṂVADĀ. Anasūyā, do you know why Śakuntalā is so fascinated with that jasmine?

ANASŪYĀ. I can't imagine—do tell.

PRIYAṂVADĀ. She's thinking—'Just as the jasmine has found a suitable tree, so may I too find a suitable husband.'

ŚAKUNTALĀ. Isn't that *your* heart's desire?

[*She pours from the pitcher*

KING. Indeed, if only she could be the child of the brahmin holy man and a woman of a different class.* But why should I worry?

Truly, if my noble heart desires her, (20)
That makes her fit to be a prince's wife,
For the wise man trusts his heart
To lead him out of doubt.

Still, I must find out the truth about her.

ŚAKUNTALĀ [*in confusion*]. Aiee! Disturbed by my watering, a bee has flown out of the jasmine into my face!

[*She shows every sign of being attacked by a bee*

KING [*longingly*]. Wonderful! Even this threat enhances her charm:

Where the bee flies (20a)
There fly her eyes,
Beneath her lovely knitted brows,
She darts an ardent glance,
Inspired by fear.
Mere practice, for on other days,
Such looks shall match a lover's gaze
In pure desire.

Ah, honey-maker, fanned by her lashes, (21)
You brush her tender lids, or hover
In her ear, murmuring a secret
That is yours alone. But, best of wishes,
You brave her flailing hands, and from that under-
Lip you steal the concentrated power
Of love.
And so you win her,
While I am stalled,
In supposition.

ŚAKUNTALĀ. So bold, it won't give up. Over here—but no, it's following! Friends, save me from this obstinate rogue.

ANASŪYĀ AND PRIYAṂVADĀ [*smiling*]. Who are *we* to protect you? Call on Duṣyanta for help—everyone knows ascetic groves are protected by the king.

KING. A chance to show myself. Don't be afr- [*mutters aside as he breaks off*]. No, no, that's too obvious, they'll know who I am. I'll do it this way instead . . .

ŚAKUNTALĀ [*taking another step and glancing around*]. How! It's still after me!

KING [*quickly stepping forward*]. Ha!

What oaf dares bring such discord and confusion (22)
Into the tender lives of hermit girls,
When the entire region enjoys the protection
Of the chastising Paurava king?*

[*On the* KING'S *appearance, they all become agitated*

ANASŪYĀ. My lord, it's nothing serious. Our friend was bothered by a bee, and became agitated. [*She points out* ŚAKUNTALĀ

KING [*going up to* ŚAKUNTALĀ]. Is your religious practice going well?

[ŚAKUNTALĀ *stands, speechless in consternation*

ANASŪYĀ. It is indeed, now that we have a distinguished guest. Śakuntalā dear, run to the hermitage and fetch some fruit and refreshments to offer our visitor. We can use this water for his feet.

KING. Ladies, your kind words alone are all the refreshment I require.

PRIYAṂVADĀ. Then at least, sir, rest yourself by taking a seat in the cool shade of this spreading tree.

KING. But you too must be feeling tired after all your work. Join me for a while, won't you?

ANASŪYĀ. Śakuntalā, dear, it's only proper that we look after our guest. Sit down here with us.

[*They all sit down*

ŚAKUNTALĀ [*to herself*]. But how can it have happened that, simply at the sight of this man, I am shaken with a passion so at odds with the religious life?

KING [*looking at them together*]. Ah, ladies! What a charming friendship, and between such equals in youth and beauty.

PRIYAṂVADĀ [*aside*]. Anasūyā, who *is* he? He speaks so sweetly and with such charm, he seems to have such majesty, and yet there's an air of mystery about him.

ANASŪYĀ. My dear, I can't wait to find out either—I'm going to ask him directly. [*Aloud*] Your Honour's fine speech makes me bold to ask—which line of royal sages is graced by Your Honour? . . . And what is the name of that country whose people are now pining because of their separation from you? . . . And why have you subjected your most refined self to the trouble of visiting our hermitage?*

ŚAKUNTALĀ [*to herself*]. Calm yourself: Anasūyā is asking everything you'd like to know.

KING [*to himself*]. Shall I make myself known now, or shall I remain incognito? Well . . . let me put it like this. [*Aloud*] Lady, I have been appointed by the Paurava king as Minister for Religious Welfare. And in that capacity I've come to this sacred forest to ensure your rituals are not obstructed in any way.

ANASŪYĀ. Now the performers of religious rites have a minister!

[ŚAKUNTALĀ *displays all the embarrassment of erotic attraction**

ANASŪYĀ AND PRIYAṂVADĀ [*noting the expressions of the other two, aside to* ŚAKUNTALĀ]. Dear Śakuntalā, if father were here with us today . . .

ŚAKUNTALĀ. What would happen?

ANASŪYĀ AND PRIYAṂVADĀ. He would make sure that this distinguished guest had everything he wanted—and that includes his most valuable treasure.

ŚAKUNTALĀ. That's enough! You've got some silly notion in your heads. I'm not listening to another word.

KING. Now I too have something to ask—about your friend.

ANASŪYĀ AND PRIYAṂVADĀ. Sir, it's an honour to be asked by you.

KING. It is public knowledge that Lord Kaṇva lives in a state of perpetual chastity—and yet your friend is his daughter. How is that?

ANASŪYĀ. I'll tell you, sir. There's a certain very powerful royal sage, whose family name is Kauśika . . .*

KING. Yes, I've heard of him—go on.

ANASŪYĀ. He's the . . . natural father of our friend, but it was Father Kaṇva who fostered her when she was abandoned, so he's her father too, you understand.

KING. 'Abandoned', you say? How very interesting. Tell me everything, from the beginning.

ANASŪYĀ. It was like this, sir. Some years ago now, that royal sage was engaged in some powerful ascetic exercises on the banks of the Gautamī river. This upset the gods, who sent the nymph Menakā to test his self-restraint.

KING. Yes, they say the gods have this fear of others practising deep meditation.* So what happened then?

ANASŪYĀ. Ah, my lord! It was the beginning of spring when he caught sight of her intoxicating body . . .

[*She breaks off modestly half-way through*

KING. I see. The upshot is, this lady's the daughter of the nymph.

ANASŪYĀ. Exactly.

KING. It all makes sense, for

How could such beauty stem from mortal birth? (23)
Does lightning strike upwards out of the earth?

[ŚAKUNTALĀ *stands looking down at her feet*

[*To himself*] My desires have a foothold at last!* But wait—what about her friend's teasing prayer for a husband? I'm undermined again.

PRIYAṂVADĀ [*smiling first at* ŚAKUNTALĀ, *then turning to face the king*]. Your Honour seems to want to say something else.

[ŚAKUNTALĀ *wags her finger at her friend*

KING. You're quite right, lady. Because I'm so eager to hear about the lives of the virtuous, there *is* another question I should like to ask.

PRIYAṂVADĀ. Don't hesitate, my lord—there are no bars to what you may ask an ascetic.

KING. Then tell me this about your friend:

How long will she keep her love-starved hermit vows— (24)
Till she changes them for the marriage kind?
Or will she live forever among these hinds,
Doe-eyed among her beloved does?

PRIYAṂVADĀ. Sir, she is not a free agent, especially in the matter of religious duty. But it is her guardian's intention to give her in marriage to a suitable husband.

KING [*to himself*]. There's no great difficulty in that.

Heart, give in to your desire— (25)
This removes all doubt.
What you supposed a fire
Is a jewel that may be felt.

ŚAKUNTALĀ [*as though very angry*]. Anasūyā, I'm going now!

ANASŪYĀ. Why?

ŚAKUNTALĀ. I'm off to the venerable Gautamī* to report Priyaṃvadā here for talking such nonsense.

ANASŪYĀ. But my dear friend, it's simply not done to neglect the hospitality of a distinguished guest and trip off just as the fancy takes you.

[ŚAKUNTALĀ *sets off without replying*

KING [*wanting to catch hold of her, but then restraining himself*]. Ah, the workings of a lover's mind are almost actions in themselves! For I

Seemed to go, and yet (26)
I never moved towards her—
Nice manners suddenly disabling
My pursuit of the forest sage's daughter.

PRIYAṂVADĀ [*holding* ŚAKUNTALĀ *back*]. Darling, it's simply not proper for you to leave now.

ŚAKUNTALĀ [*frowning*]. Why ever not?

PRIYAṂVADĀ. You owe me for watering two of your trees. Repay me in kind, and so release yourself. [*So saying, she steers her back*

KING. Gracious lady, I can see that your young friend is already exhausted from watering. Look how

From heaving up the pot, her palms are raw, (27)
Her shoulders stoop,
Her breath is laboured and her bosom shakes,
All sifted strength.
On filmy sweat the mimosa's bloom
Slides from ear to cheek,
And as her hairband slips, those cobalt locks
Flow round her submerged hand
Like water round a rock.

So let me discharge her debt for her.

[*He offers her his signet-ring. Reading the inscription on the seal, the girls stare at each other*

KING. Don't misunderstand. This is a gift from the king—and I, as you know, am the king's man.

PRIYAMVADĀ. In that case, it's not right for the ring to leave your finger. She is already free of her debt by Your Honour's word. [*Laughing a little*] Dear Śakuntalā, you have been released by His Honour's compassion—or should I say by the king himself? So now you must go . . .

ŚAKUNTALĀ [*to herself*]. If I have the strength. [*Aloud*] Who are you to release or detain me?

KING [*watching* ŚAKUNTALĀ; *to himself*]. Can it be that she feels for me what I feel for her? Then perhaps I have a real chance, for:

What though she doesn't answer me directly? (28)
What though she doesn't look me in the face?
When I speak, she is quiet attention,
When I gaze, evasive grace.

OFF-STAGE VOICE. Quick! Quick, you ascetics! Get ready to save the animals in our sacred grove! King Duṣyanta is somewhere near at hand, revelling in the chase.

Dust beaten upwards by his horses' hooves, (29)
Dust, like a locust cloud,
Unfurls and swarms
On the trees
On the half-dry tunics—
Dust red as the dying sun.

Worse still:

The penances we strove to execute are incomplete— (30)
Panicked by the chariots, scattering the grazing does,
Creepers like broken lariats snaking round its feet,
An elephant obliterates the sacred grove.
Obstruction incarnate, on its tusk
It pulps with juddering blows
A saplings's skewered trunk.

[*At this, the women become agitated*

KING [*to himself*]. Ah! My people are invading the grove trying to find me! I must go straight back.

ANASŪYĀ AND PRIYAṂVADĀ. Sir, we're frightened by this talk of an elephant. Please allow us to return to our hut.

KING [*agitated himself*]. By all means go, ladies. In the meantime, I'll do my best to make sure no harm comes to the ashram.

[*They all get up*

ANASŪYĀ AND PRIYAṂVADĀ. Sir, our hospitality has been so poor that we hardly dare to ask Your Honour to visit us again.

KING. That's not true. Besides, just to be with you ladies is hospitality enough.

ŚAKUNTALĀ. Anasūyā! I've spiked my foot on a blade of grass . . . And now my blouse is snagged on a branch. Wait while I free myself!

[*Using this pretence to remain gazing at the king*, ŚAKUNTALĀ *finally leaves with her friends*

KING. Suddenly, the city doesn't seem so attractive. I'll link up with my followers and camp just outside this sacred grove. The truth is, I can't get Śakuntalā out of my head.

My body forges on, my restless mind streams back— (31)
A silken banner borne against the wind.

[*Exit the* KING

ACT 2

Enter the VIDŪṢAKA* (MĀDHAVYA), *out of sorts.*

VIDŪṢAKA [*sighing*]. Oh, I've had quite enough of this sporty king's company. On we go through this endless forest, chasing echoes: 'Over here—a stag!' 'Over there—a boar!' 'On your tail—a tiger!' It's midday, the sun's hammering my head, the leaves have shrivelled from the heat and there's no shade to speak of. We drink the tepid water of mountain streams, famous for its bitter aftertaste. The secret ingredient? Stale leaves. There are no proper meal times, and there's nothing on the menu anyway, except meat, roasted on a spit, or, for a change, roast meat. I'm so racked and reassembled from riding all day, I can't even get a decent night's sleep. Then what happens? Before the sun's even shown its face, I'm woken by those bastard huntsmen, roaring like barbarians as they fence off some part of the forest to dispose of its bird population . . . So, all in all, you would think suffering had done well enough out of me to clear off while the going's good. But no such luck—now the ulcer's sprouted a boil. Yesterday, we were trailing behind, and what happens? My friendly misfortune follows His Highness into an ashram [when he's supposed to be chasing a deer] and introduces him to one Śakuntalā, an ascetic's daughter. And since then he hasn't given a thought to returning to the city . . . He was up all night meditating on her . . . What can I do about it? First of all, get hold of him as soon as he's finished his morning ablutions. [*Turning and looking*] Ah, here comes my friend now, surrounded by his attendant girls* garlanded in wild flowers and waving their bows about. Well, I'll just stand here, clamped to my own disabled body, so to speak. Which, if nothing else, allows me to get some rest.

[*Stands supporting himself on a wooden staff*

Enter the KING, *surrounded by his* ATTENDANTS.

KING. She's hard to win, my love— (1)
But while I sense the same fire burns in her

I'm happy to persist,
For just a hint of mutual passion's
Bliss,
This side of consummation.

[*Smiling*] So the lover's mocked, misreading his own feelings in his darling's heart.

When she looked lovingly (2)
 at someone or something else,
When she moved with heavy hips
 as though slowed down by love,
When she spoke so sharply
 to the friend who tried to halt her,
I read all these as secret signs
For me alone—
Such is the power that lovers have
To make the world their own.

VIDŪṢAKA [*rooted there in the same way*]. Ahem! Friend! My arms and legs are cast, so I shall simply give you a vocal salutation: 'May you always triumph, My Lord! May you always triumph!'

KING. What's brought on this sudden disability?

VIDŪṢAKA. What! You poke me in the eye yourself, and then ask me why it's watering?

KING. I can't say I follow you.

VIDŪṢAKA. Ah, friend! Does the reed in the stream bend with the elegance of a hunchback* through its own weight alone, or through the force of the current?

KING. Obviously, through the force of the current.

VIDŪṢAKA. For me, you are the current.

KING. How so?

VIDŪṢAKA. Because you're neglecting affairs of state to live the life of a woodman in a hole like this. The truth is, my joints have been shaken apart—I've been crippled by this endless wild-beast chase. So be nice to me, won't you, and give it a rest—just for a day?

KING [*aside*]. Well, that's a matter of opinion . . . But, in fact, thinking of Kaṇva's daughter is enough to make even me sick of the chase. For:

I've not the heart to bend this bow and aim this shaft (3)
At those very hinds with whom my dearest lived
And somehow learned, by art or mutual graft,
That limpid gaze.

VIDŪṢAKA [*watching the king's expression*]. His Majesty is clearly muttering away with something else in mind. And I was just 'crying in the wilderness', so to speak.

KING [*smiling*]. What something else? I was just standing thinking that I shouldn't ignore a friend's advice.

VIDŪṢAKA. May you live for ever!

[*He makes to leave*

KING. Just wait a moment, my friend. I haven't finished what I was saying yet.

VIDŪṢAKA. Command me, sir!

KING. Once you're rested, I'd appreciate your help in a little untaxing business.

VIDŪṢAKA. To eat some sweeties? O, then I accept with relish.*

KING. I'll tell you later. Hello! Who's there?

Enter the DOORKEEPER.

DOORKEEPER [*bowing*]. Your Lordship's servant.

KING. Raivataka, just ask the General to step in, will you.

DOORKEEPER. I shall, sir.

[*Exiting and returning immediately with the* GENERAL

There's the master, looking this way, just dying to give his orders. You should approach him, Your Honour.

GENERAL [*looking towards the* KING]. Well, it may be considered a vice,* but for the commander-in-chief the hunt has produced nothing but good. For the king's

Body is latent power, (4)
Leathery from the bow-string's friction,
Sun-resistant, sweat-free, thin but muscular—
His Majesty has the torso of a wild mountain tusker!

[*Approaching*] Victory! Victory to Your Majesty! We have surrounded the forest beasts, and now we await your orders.

KING. Mādhavya's sermon against hunting has dampened my enthusiasm for the chase.

GENERAL [*aside to* VIDŪṢAKA]. You keep up the opposition, friend, while I humour His Majesty. [*Aloud*] Let this fool chunter on. But surely His Majesty himself provides the best evidence:

Your waist wasted from fat to muscle, (5)
Your body freed to swerve and tumble,
You peer into the angry, fearful minds
Of creatures in extremis,
Honing your archer's skill
On fast and fleeting targets.
Is this a vice?
Don't believe it!
Nothing beats it!

VIDŪṢAKA. Bah! Enough of this you motivator! His Majesty has come to himself. But since you like it so much, *you* go roaming from forest to forest and, with luck, you'll fall into the mouth of some ancient and patient bear, who's been waiting fifty years for just such a delicacy as a man's nose.

KING. My dear General, I can hardly approve of your sentiments when we're camped so close to a hermitage. So for the present:

Let buffalo cloud the pool with their restless horns, (6)
Let deer chew the cud in crowded shadows,
Let the boar root up in peace the weed-clogged ponds,
And let this, my unstrung bow, rest until tomorrow.

GENERAL. As your lordship pleases.

KING. So, fetch back those beaters who've gone ahead, and make sure there's no chance my soldiers will disturb the penance grove. For understand

That those peaceful ascetics are sunstones*—cool enough (7)
Until their inner fire, ignited by some fire in you,
Catches, and consumes you, through and through.

GENERAL. As my lord commands.

VIDŪṢAKA. So much for your talk of action!

[*Exit* GENERAL

KING [*looking at his* ATTENDANTS]. Take off your hunting gear. And you, Raivataka, make use of yourself.

ATTENDANTS. As Your Majesty commands.

[*Exit* ATTENDANTS

VIDŪṢAKA. Now you've got rid of the flies, my lord, rest yourself on that rock beneath the tree. We could all do with some shade.

KING. Lead the way.

VIDŪṢAKA. Come, my lord.

[*They walk around and sit down*

KING. Mādhavya, you'll never know why you were given eyes until you've seen the one thing really worth seeing.

VIDŪṢAKA. Is that so? I thought you were standing right in front of me.

KING. Everyone considers himself attractive. But I'm referring to that jewel of the ashram, Śakuntalā.

VIDŪṢAKA [*to himself*]. Right! I'll take the wind out of his sails. [*Aloud*] Oh I see, my friend—you've set your heart on a celibate hermit girl?

KING. Ignoramus!

Why do men turn and gaze (7a)
When the crescent moon
Cuts the evening haze?

Anyway, friend, a Paurava never hankers after forbidden fruit.

One parent was a nymph and one a kingly sage, (8)
But like a jasmine torn from its native stem
To land in safety on an arka's pliant leaf,*
She was abandoned—only to find home again
In a forest, with a priestly sage.

VIDŪṢAKA [*grinning*]. For a man who's overdosed on dates, the sourness of the tamarind has its attractions—and you, having gorged yourself on beautiful women, want this girl.

KING. You can only talk like that because you haven't seen her.

VIDŪṢAKA. Well, she must be very special indeed to get you so excited.

KING. Friend, I can only ask this:

Did the great Creator first draw her in a masterpiece, (9)
And then touch life into his art?
Or did he make her in his mind alone,
Drawing on beauty's every part?
No—considering her singular perfection
And her maker's true omnipotence,
I suppose her some quite unique creation
In femininity's treasure house.

VIDŪṢAKA. That sounds like bad news for beautiful women in general.

KING. It seems to me she is

A blossom yet unsmelt, (10)
A tender shoot unpinched,
A gem uncut,
Untasted, fresh-fermented honey-wine,
The fruit of proper actions
Still intact—
A beauty without fault or flaw.
But who among us here
Is destined to enjoy her,
Is still unclear.

VIDŪṢAKA. In that case, my lord, you must rescue her quickly, before she falls into the hands of some smooth ascetic, his head plastered with iṅgudi oil.

KING. The lady is a minor, and her guardian is currently away from home.

VIDŪṢAKA. Can you tell anything from the way she looks at you?

KING. Hermit girls are by nature very modest. Still:

As I tried to catch her eye, she dropped her gaze, (11)
And smiled,
As though at something else.
So love's impulse, modestly restrained,
Turned below the surface,
Part silhouette, part flame

VIDŪṢAKA. Perhaps you expected her to jump into your lap the moment she clapped eyes on you?

KING. No, but as she was setting off with her friends, she very nearly—with all due modesty—revealed the strength of her feelings. In

Going just a pace or two she lagged (12)
Behind—that delicate girl—for no clear reason,
Claiming she'd cut her foot on a spike of darbha.
Then, 'freeing' her tunic—though hardly snagged—
From tangled branches, she turned in my direction
And gazed with what seemed like ardour.

VIDŪṢAKA. Then send out for a hamper! I can see that you've turned the penance-grove into a pleasure-garden!

KING. Friend, some of the ascetics have recognized me; so if I'm to visit the ashram again I need a new excuse. Any ideas?

VIDŪṢAKA. What special excuse do you kings need? Just walk in and order them to give up a sixth of their wild rice in tax.

KING. Fool! The tax these ascetics pay is of quite another kind, and much more valuable than mountains of pearls. Don't you see?

What kings raise from society (13)
Falls away,
But what these forest-dwellers make through penance
Can never decay.

VOICES OFF-STAGE. This is the place we're looking for!

KING [*listening*]. Such deep, calm voices! They can only belong to ascetics.

DOORKEEPER [*entering*]. Victory, victory to my lord! There are two young seers waiting at the entrance.

KING. Then show them in at once.

DOORKEEPER. I'll bring them now.

[*He exits and returns with the two young* SEERS

This way, please, sirs.

[*They both stare at the* KING

FIRST SEER. Ah, doesn't he look brilliant, and at the same time he inspires such confidence! But you'd expect that in a king who's virtually a seer himself. For:

Like an ascetic, he has chosen a special way of living (14)
For the good of all;
Protecting his subjects, he earns continuous merit
Through self-control;
Bards in harmony praise him to heaven
With the holy titles 'sage' and 'king'.

SECOND SEER. Gautama, is this that same Duṣyanta who is the companion of Indra?

FIRST SEER. The very same.

SECOND SEER. Then:

Little wonder he alone rules the entire world (15)
To the margins of the storm-dark sea,
His arms as broad and strong as the beam
That bars a city gate.
Aided by his tensile bow and Indra's bolt,
The gods anticipate
Nothing less than victory
In their assault
On the demon host.

BOTH SEERS [*approaching*]. Be victorious, indeed, my king!

KING [*rising from his seat*]. I salute you both.

BOTH SEERS. And our best wishes to you! [*They offer him fruit*

KING [*accepting it with a bow*]. What can I do for you?

BOTH SEERS. The inhabitants of the ashram have learnt that Your Honour is here, and they have a request to make of you.

KING. Their wish is my command.

BOTH SEERS. They say that, owing to the absence of the great and revered sage Kaṇva, evil spirits are disrupting their rituals, and so they ask that you should come with your driver and protect the ashram for the next few nights.

KING. It's an honour to be asked.

VIDŪṢAKA [*aside*]. This couldn't be better if you'd planned it yourself.

KING [*smiling*]. Raivataka, tell my driver I want him to bring the chariot here, along with my bow.

DOORKEEPER. Whatever you command. [*He withdraws*

BOTH SEERS [*with delight*].

And so you are at one with your ancestors: (16)
For all the descendants of Puru are initiates
In that great sacrifice which protects
The afflicted and alleviates
Their pain.

KING [*bowing*]. Please go ahead. I'll be close behind you.

BOTH SEERS. Be victorious, lord! [*They withdraw*

KING. Mādhavya, are you still curious to see Śakuntalā?

VIDŪṢAKA. At first I was overflowing, but this talk of spirits has helped to mop me up.

KING. Don't be afraid—I shall be right next to you the entire time.

VIDŪṢAKA. So you'll spirit the spirits away from me?

DOORKEEPER [*entering*]. The chariot is yoked and awaits your departure to victory, my lord. But Karabhaka has just arrived from the city with a message from the Queen Mother.

KING [*respectfully*]. What, sent by our mother herself?

DOORKEEPER. Just so.

KING. Then show him in.

DOORKEEPER. As you command.

[*Exits and returns with* KARABHAKA

Here is His Majesty. You may approach him.

KARABHAKA. Victory to my lord, victory! This is the request of Her Majesty: four days from now the ritual fast to safeguard the son's succession begins. Her Majesty considers it essential that you, sire, should be present on that occasion.

KING. I have to weigh my duty to the ascetics against the request of a revered parent—and neither can be ignored. So what's to be done?

VIDŪṢAKA. Hover in the middle, like Triśaṅku.*

KING. Seriously, I'm in a dilemma:

Because they're in quite different places, (17)
My mind divides between these two,
Like a river when a rock displaces
Its seamless flow.

[*Pondering*] Mother certainly thinks of you as another son, my friend. So . . . go to her—explain how I'm preoccupied with my duty to help the ascetics—and then play the son's part in the ritual for Her Majesty yourself.

VIDŪṢAKA. But you don't really think I'm scared of spirits, do you?

KING [*smiling*]. That's impossible, isn't it? You're a brahmin.

VIDŪṢAKA. Just for now, I should like to travel as though I were really the king's younger brother.

KING. Actually, I will send my retinue back with you. It won't do to disrupt the hermitage again.

VIDŪṢAKA [*proudly*]. Then make way for the heir-apparent!

KING [*to himself*]. To describe this chattering brahmin as indiscreet is to drown in understatement. Once he's back among the women in the palace, there'll be nothing to stop him gossiping about my affair. Let's see . . . I'll tell him this. [*Taking the Vidūṣaka by the hand, he speaks aloud*] Friend, you must understand that I am only going to the ashram out of respect for the seers. I don't really feel anything for the hermit girl. After all:

Think of the gulf that divides a king like me (18)
From a girl raised with fawns,
Innocent in the ways of passion.
Remember too, my friend, what's said in jest
Shouldn't be taken in some other fashion.

VIDŪṢAKA. I understand.

[*They all leave*

ACT 3

Enter an ASSISTANT *of the sacrificer* (KAṆVA), *carrying kusha grass for the sacrifice.*

ASSISTANT. Ah, how powerful King Duṣyanta is! He had only to enter the ashram for everything that obstructed our rituals to fall away.

What need to fit the arrow to the bow (1)
When his reverberating string alone
Disperses with its angry hum
The demon foe?

I must take this grass for the priests to spread on the altar. [*Walking about, seeing someone, and speaking aloud*] Priyaṃvadā, who is that ointment for? And the lotus-leaf fibre? [*Listening*] What do you say? That Śakuntalā has gone down with heatstroke, and it's to soothe her limbs? Then spare no pains, for she is the very life breath of our patriarch, Father Kaṇva. I'll send Gautamī with some of the sacrificial water—it will help to cool her.

[*Exit* ASSISTANT

Enter the KING, *lovesick.*

KING [*sighing pensively*].

I know the strength of penance and I know (2)
The lady's subject to a different power,
But like moisture in an upturned flower
My heart is trapped, and lacks the means to go.

Great God of love, why am I in torment, when your arrows are nothing but flowers? [*Recollecting*] But of course!

Though he reduced you to ash,* (2a)
Śiva's fury still burns in your veins
Like submarine fire.
How else, God of desire,
Do you cause me such pains?

But you and the moon are one in the way you betray the trust that lovers give you.

For they say— (3)
Your shafts are flowers, and lunar rays are cool,
But those are half-truths for a man like me,
When the moon, for all its frozen marrow,
Darts solar beams, and every floral spray
Hides a diamond arrow.

And yet:

I'll love the God of Love (4)
If all my mental anguish
Stems from nothing but this lady
And her almond eyes.

[*Walking in a depressed state*] Now the rites are over, and I'm no longer needed by the priests, how shall I revive myself? [*Sighing*] I can't—unless I see my love, my only refuge. I shall seek her out. [*Looking at the sun*] It's now the hottest time of day. Śakuntalā usually spends it with her friends in the bowers of vines on the banks of the Mālinī—and that's where I'll go. [*Walking around and feeling the touch of the breeze*] Ah! This place is cooled by the most magical breezes!

Moist with the river's spray, (5)
The lotus-scented wind
Sighs to soothe my love burnt limbs.

[*Walking around and looking*] Yes! Śakuntalā must be nearby. For:

At the entrance to this bower (6)
Her footprints tread the sandy soil
Toe-light, heel-heavy, canted
By the tilt and weight
Of her body's delicate power.

I'll just peer through the branches. [*Filled with joy*] Ah! My eyes are in paradise! For here is my heart's desire, resting on a smooth rock covered in flowers, attended by her friends. Let me listen to them.

He stands watching. ŚAKUNTALĀ *appears as described, with her two friends.*

ANASŪYĀ AND PRIYAṂVADĀ [*fanning her affectionately*]. Dearest Śakuntalā, doesn't the breeze from this lotus leaf make you feel better?

ŚAKUNTALĀ. Are you fanning me, darlings?

[*The friends glance at each other in alarm*

KING. Śakuntalā seems to be very ill. [*Pondering*] Now, is it the heat, or is it the heart, as it is with me? [*Gazing with longing*] But there's really no question:

Her breasts are smeared with lotus balm, (7)
Her fibre bracelet slips her wrist,*
Her body's racked—and lovely still,
The summer sears her—but so does love,
And love with greater skill.

PRIYAṂVADĀ [*aside*]. Anasūyā, ever since she first saw the king, Śakuntalā has been terribly restless. Perhaps he is the cause of her fever?

ANASŪYĀ. Yes, I was wondering about that as well. It's time to question her. [*Aloud*] My dear, I have to ask you something. You seem to be in a lot of pain.

ŚAKUNTALĀ [*raising herself a little*]. What do you want to say to me, friend?

ANASŪYĀ. Dear Śakuntalā, we're quite ignorant in the ways of love. But if the stories are to be believed, then it seems to me you're feeling exactly what women in love are said to feel. So tell us the real cause of your pain—nothing can be cured until it's been properly diagnosed.

KING. So I didn't just imagine it! Anasūyā echoes my thought.

ŚAKUNTALĀ [*to herself*]. It's all too much—I can't talk about it.

PRIYAṂVADĀ. Dear Śakuntalā, Anasūyā's quite right: you must face up to your illness. Why—you're fading away in front of our eyes. All that survives of you is a beautiful shadow.

KING. That's nothing less than the truth. For:

Her cheeks are drawn, her bosom shrinks, (8)
Her waist contracts, her shoulders stoop,
Her colour drains. Love strikes her down—
A beauty sad as spring's young leaves,
Shrivelled in the furnace of the summer's breeze.

ŚAKUNTALĀ. Darlings, who else could I tell but you? But it will upset you.

ANASŪYĀ AND PRIYAṂVADĀ. That's exactly why we've asked you. When you share your unhappiness with your closest friends, you make it bearable.

KING.

They share her every joy and sorrow— (9)
She'll tell them why she's sick at heart.
She seemed to gaze at me with longing,
But now I'm full of doubt.

ŚAKUNTALĀ. Friends, from the very moment I saw that royal sage who protects the hermitage— [*She breaks off in embarrassment*

ANASŪYĀ AND PRIYAṂVADĀ. Do go on, my dear.

ŚAKUNTALĀ. From that moment, I've been filled with longing for him . . . And that's why I'm in this state.

KING [*joyfully*]. I've heard what I needed to hear.

Love, that laid me low, has pulled me up again— (10)
Just as a dark and airless day
Dispels the heat
With sudden rain.

ŚAKUNTALĀ. So, darlings, if you think it proper, help me to the king's pity. Otherwise—prepare my body for the fire.

KING. Her words put a fire to doubt.

PRIYAṂVADĀ [*aside*]. Anasūyā, she's so far in love, there's no time to lose. And we can hardly object to her choice—to fall for the jewel of the Puru line!

ANASŪYĀ. You're right.

PRIYAṂVADĀ [*aloud*]. My dear, how lucky, then, that your desire's at one with nature. Where should a great river wend, if not to the sea? What plant's lush enough for the jasmine to entwine, if not the mango?

KING. What wonder if the double stars of spring* do service to the crescent moon?

ANASŪYĀ. But how can we arrange what she wants with any speed or secrecy?

PRIYAṂVADĀ. Secrecy will need some thought, but speed is easy.

ANASŪYĀ. Really?

PRIYAṂVADĀ. Surely, with all those loving glances, the king has made it clear enough what he feels for her? And now he's as thin as she is from lack of sleep.

KING. Ah, yes:

Night after night tears cloud the jewels (11)
Of this, my golden bracelet's trim—
It shuttles up and down my arm, made slim
By love's cruel wastage of my bow-scarred limbs.

PRIYAṂVADĀ [*thinking*]. My dear, she must write him a love letter. Then I'll hide it in some flowers, and, pretending it's an offering blessed by the god, I'll hand it to him directly.

ANASŪYĀ. I love it—it's a most fragrant plan. But what does Śakuntalā think?

ŚAKUNTALĀ. Who am I to interfere with your plans?

PRIYAṂVADĀ. Then you must think up a love poem that will show him exactly what you're feeling.

ŚAKUNTALĀ. Very well . . . I'm thinking. But I can't help trembling at the thought—suppose he rejects me?

KING [*delighted*].

Bashful girl! The man you want (12)
Stands here, dying to fold you in his arms.
The wealth-seeker finds her, or not,
As the goddess Lakṣmī* wills,
But when she herself pursues,
Who can resist her charms?

ANASŪYĀ AND PRIYAṂVADĀ. Why do you run yourself down? Who would swathe themselves in cloth to keep off the cooling light of the autumn moon?

ŚAKUNTALĀ [*smiling*]. Well, if you insist. [*She sits and thinks*

KING. When I gaze at my beloved, my eyes forget to blink. And they are right, for:

As she composes, an eyebrow puckered in thought, (13)
Like a tendril curling on a fresh young vine,
Her face, her downy cheek sing out her wish:
'I am his—and would that he were mine.'

ŚAKUNTALĀ. Friends, I've thought of a song, but how can I write it down?

PRIYAṂVADĀ. Use your nails—etch the letter into this lotus leaf. It's as soft as the plumage in a parrot's breast.

ŚAKUNTALĀ [*doing as directed*]. Friends, listen to this. Does it work, or not?

ANASŪYĀ AND PRIYAṂVADĀ. We're listening!

ŚAKUNTALĀ.

I cannot say I know your mind, (14)
But day and night the god of love
Injects that pain through all my limbs,
Which you prepared—ah sweet unkind—
I cannot say I know your mind.

KING [*revealing himself suddenly*].

Slender lady, you should know (15)
That same love which tortures you

Consumes me quite—
The sun, that merely dulls the lotus' glow,
Engulfs the moon in azure light.

ANASŪYĀ AND PRIYAṂVADĀ [*seeing him and arising with delight*]. Welcome to our wish, which has arrived post-haste, in the person of the beloved himself!

[ŚAKUNTALĀ *tries to rise*

KING. Don't get up!

Limbs cushioned on flowers— (16)
Bruised lotuses, fragrant
But listless with pain—
Should conserve their powers,
And treat stale custom with proper disdain.

ANASŪYĀ. Then let the king sit down—on this stone bench.

[*The* KING *sits down next to* ŚAKUNTALĀ, *who remains there, embarrassed*

PRIYAṂVADĀ. Your love for each other is obvious. But my love for my friend . . . Yet, perhaps it doesn't really need to be said.

KING. My dear, don't hold back now if you're going to regret it later.

PRIYAṂVADĀ. They say it is the king's duty to relieve the pain of those who live in his realm.

KING. There is no higher calling.

PRIYAṂVADĀ. Well then, our dear friend has been reduced to this condition through her love for you. So, if you would save her life, you must take her under your protection.

KING. We are of one mind, my dear—and everything you say does me honour.

ŚAKUNTALĀ [*looking at* PRIYAṂVADĀ]. Darling, why are you troubling the king, when he must be longing to return to the women of the palace?

KING: Bewitching lady, soul of my soul:

You give the final thrust to one already felled (17)
By Kāma's dart,* if you suppose
My wounded heart could be impelled
To break your trust
And love another.

ANASŪYĀ. Lord, it's said that kings have many wives. You won't, I hope, treat our dear friend here in such a way that, for the rest of her life, she'll be a source of grief to her family.

KING. Lady, what more can I say than this:

Kings indeed have many wives, (18)
But my succession
Rests on two alone:
The sea-engirdled earth,*
And your dear friend.

ANASŪYĀ AND PRIYAṂVADĀ. We're happy now.

PRIYAṂVADĀ [*casting a glance*]. Anasūyā, that fawn is looking all over the place for its mother. Let's take it to her!

[*Both start to leave*

ŚAKUNTALĀ. Friends! Come back! One of you—I'm unguarded!

ANASŪYĀ AND PRIYAṂVADĀ. With the *world's* guardian at your side?

[*They leave*

ŚAKUNTALĀ. Why have they gone?

KING. Don't be alarmed. I shall look after you. Command me love:

Will moist air, stirred by the fans of lotus fronds (19)
Suffice to cool and refresh you?
Or shall I massage, in my lap, your lotus-reddened feet?

ŚAKUNTALĀ. I must not offend those I respect!

[*Rising as though wanting to leave*

KING. Dazzling lady, the day is still hot, and where, in your state,

Will you go in this shimmering heat, (20)
Exposing limbs made frail by love,

When lotus leaves could shade you from above,
And blossoms revive you in some cool retreat?

[*He forces her to turn around*

ŚAKUNTALĀ. Puru king, restrain yourself! I too may be consumed by love, but I'm not free to give myself to you.

KING. Timid fawn—don't worry about your elders! The father of your family knows the law, and he shall find no fault in what you've done.* Besides:

You wouldn't be the first royal sage's daughter (21)
To take a prince for love—
And receive her father's blessings later.

ŚAKUNTALĀ. Let me go now. I need to ask my friends' advice.

KING. Yes. I shall release you—

ŚAKUNTALĀ. When?

KING. When?

When, like a bee, I kiss the bud of your unbruised lip (22)
And flood my thirsting mouth with nectar.

[*With these words, he tries to raise her face.* ŚAKUNTALĀ *evades him with a dance*

OFF-STAGE VOICE. Red goose, take leave of your gander.* Night is falling!

ŚAKUNTALĀ [*agitated*]. Puru Lord, the venerable Gautamī is certainly coming this way to enquire after my health. Hide amongst these branches.

KING. Very well.

[*He hides himself and waits*

GAUTAMĪ *enters with a pot in her hand, accompanied by* ANASŪYĀ *and* PRIYAṂVADĀ.

ANASŪYĀ AND PRIYAṂVADĀ. This way, this way, Mother Gautamī!

GAUTAMĪ [*approaching* ŚAKUNTALĀ]. Child, are you feeling any better?

ŚAKUNTALĀ. Noble Mother, I do believe that I have taken a turn for the better.

GAUTAMĪ. With this water from the sacrifice your body shall be released from pain. [*She sprinkles* ŚAKUNTALĀ'S *head*] Child, the day is ending—it's time to go back to the hut. Come now . . .

ŚAKUNTALĀ [*aside*]. Heart, when what you most desired was within your grasp, why was it that you still couldn't overcome your shyness? So now you'll pay the price and suffer the pain of separation and regret. [*Taking another step, and speaking aloud*] O bower of creepers that so relieved my suffering, farewell—may we soon be reunited and enjoy each other again!

[*Exit* ŚAKUNTALĀ *sorrowfully, with the others*

KING [*going back to where he was, with a sigh*]. Oh, the barriers between desire and its fulfilment!

Since I managed to raise her beautiful face, (23)
Why didn't I kiss her?—
Her head was almost on my shoulder,
Her tapering fingers brushed her lower lip,
Muffling her own words of censure.

What shall I do? Go? Or linger a while in this bower, where my love rested herself, but which she has now deserted? [*Looking all around*]

Here, on this stone, printed in flowers, (24)
Is the trace of her body;
Here, on a lotus, etched by her nails,
A lover's fading letter;
Here, slipped from her wrist,
A lotus-fibre bangle—
Mementoes of her that rivet my gaze,
And delay my departure,
Though the arbour is empty,
And I am alone.

VOICE IN THE AIR. King!

Like thunderclouds in ochre light, (25)
Carnivorous demons curl and swarm,
And mass against the evening rite.

KING. Yes—I'm on my way.

[*The* KING *leaves*

ACT 4

ANASŪYĀ *and* PRIYAṂVADĀ *enter, gathering flowers.*

ANASŪYĀ. Priyaṃvadā, Śakuntalā's secret marriage has worked out so well—and to such a very suitable husband—yet I can't stop worrying.

PRIYAṂVADĀ. Why?

ANASŪYĀ. Now the king has finished the sacrifice and been released by the priests, he'll return to his capital. And once he's there among the women of the court, who can say whether he'll remember what's happened in the forest?

PRIYAṂVADĀ. Don't worry! Such men don't belie their appearance. I'm more concerned about what Father Kaṇva will do when he hears the news.

ANASŪYĀ. He'll give his approval.

PRIYAṂVADĀ. What makes you think that?

ANASŪYĀ. What does any father want most in the world? To marry his daughter to a person of quality. So if fate conspires to save him the trouble . . .

PRIYAṂVADĀ [*looking at the basket of flowers*]. My dear, we've collected enough flowers now to perform the daily offering.

ANASŪYĀ. Shouldn't we also offer something to the goddess who has blessed Śakuntalā with a happy marriage?

PRIYAṂVADĀ. I'm seeing to it now.

[*They continue the rite*

OFF-STAGE VOICE. Hello! I am here!

ANASŪYĀ [*listening*]. My dear, that sounds like a visitor announcing himself.

PRIYAṂVADĀ. Isn't Śakuntalā near the hut?

ANASŪYĀ. Yes, but she's so distracted these days. We'd better make do with the flowers we've got—

OFF-STAGE VOICE. So, you slight a guest, do you?*

That man whose brilliance (1)
Robs your thought of everything, including me,
A great ascetic fired by penance—
That man, though prompted,
Shall not remember you at all,
Like a drunken sot, who cannot recall
What he said in his cups the night before.

PRIYAṂVADĀ. Ah! What a disaster! Absent-minded Śakuntalā has offended someone she should have welcomed. [*Looking ahead*] And not just anyone—it's the great sage Durvāsas—short-tempered's not the word! Now he's cursed her, spun on his heel, and shot off like a flaming arrow!

ANASŪYĀ. Who else but fire himself should burn? Quick! Throw yourself at his feet and make him come back! I'll prepare him a water offering.

PRIYAṂVADĀ. I'll do my best! [*Exits*

ANASŪYĀ [*stumbles after taking a step*]. Ah! More haste . . . There goes the flower-basket.

[*She collects up the flowers*

PRIYAṂVADĀ [*entering*]. O my dear, he has such a cruel nature. No one can move him. But I did manage to extract just a sliver of compassion.

ANASŪYĀ [*smiling*]. That's a feast by his standards. What was it?

PRIYAṂVADĀ. When he refused to return, then I pleaded with him. 'Master, please forgive your daughter this one offence. It is her first, and she was ignorant of your worship's ascetic power.'

ANASŪYĀ. And then?

PRIYAṂVADĀ. 'I cannot unspeak what I have spoken, but the sight of a memento can lift the curse.' And so he vanished.

ANASŪYĀ. Now we can breathe again! As he set out, the king slipped a ring, inscribed with his own name, onto Śakuntalā's finger, as a keepsake. So when the time comes, she'll have just such a memento to hand.

PRIYAṂVADĀ. Come my dear, let's finish the rite we were performing for her.

[*They walk around*

PRIYAṂVADĀ [*looking*]. Anasūyā, just look at that! With her face cupped in her hand, our dear friend seems like a girl in a painting. She's so bound up in thoughts of her husband, she isn't even aware of herself, let alone neglected guests.

ANASŪYĀ. Priyaṃvadā, what's happened here today should go no further than us. You know how delicate our friend is. It's up to us to shield her.

PRIYAṂVADĀ. Who would sprinkle jasmine with boiling water?

[*Both exit*

Enter one of KAṆVA'*s pupils* (VIṢKAMBHAKA), *just risen from sleep.*

PUPIL (VIṢKAMBHAKA). The holy Kaṇva has just returned from his pilgrimage—and now he wants to know the hour. I'll go outside and see what's left of the night. [*Turning and looking*] Ah, it's nearly dawn!

As the moon, that lord of secret flowers, (2)
Declines behind the mountains in the west,
Dawn's charioteer streaks the eastern sky with rouge.
And so on earth, the going up and down of men
Governed by this alternation, dark with light,
Also arcs from morning into night.

And now the moon has set (3)
The lotus is a ghost
That recalls but cannot revive its light.
And so, her lover gone,
A girl is haunted by grief.

ANASŪYĀ [*throwing aside the curtain and entering. To herself*]. Even though a person innocent in the ways of the world knows little of these things, it's still clear the king has acted badly towards Śakuntalā.

PUPIL. I shall tell my teacher it's time to make the sacrifice.

[*Exits*

ANASŪYĀ. I'm up and about at the crack of dawn, but what shall I do? My hands and feet have lost the will to work their usual routine. I hope the God of Love, who offered my innocent friend to such a faithless man, is satisfied. Or is it Durvāsas's curse that makes him change? How else could the king, after everything he said, dispatch no letter in all this time? Perhaps we should send him his ring to remind him. But which of these austere and disciplined ascetics could we ask to go? Nor can I tell Father Kaṇva, now he's returned from his journey, that Śakuntalā is married to Duṣyanta and carries his child, for certainly she would be blamed in some measure. So what can be done?

PRIYAṂVADĀ [*entering with delight*]. Hurry, my dear! Hurry! We are to celebrate Śakuntalā's departure as a bride!

ANASŪYĀ. How can that be?

PRIYAṂVADĀ. Listen. I had just gone to ask Śakuntalā if she had slept well . . .

ANASŪYĀ. And?

PRIYAṂVADĀ. And as she stood there, staring modestly at her feet, I saw Father Kaṇva hugging her with delight, saying. 'The sacrificer's sight was darkened by smoke, yet, through the greatest good fortune, the offering fell straight into the fire. My dear child, I shall not grieve for you; but, this very day, I shall send you to your husband with an escort of seers. It will be like knowledge transmitted to a good pupil.'

ANASŪYĀ. But who told Father Kaṇva what had happened?

PRIYAṂVADĀ. When he entered the place where the sacrificial fire is kept, he heard a disembodied voice chanting a sacred verse.

ANASŪYĀ [*amazed*]. Saying what?

PRIYAṂVADĀ.

'Brahmin, know (4)
That, like fire in the womb of the wood,*
For the world's welfare your daughter
Bears the lustrous seed of King Duṣyanta.'

ANASŪYĀ [*hugging* PRIYAṂVADĀ]. Darling, this is such wonderful news! But bitter-sweet—Śakuntalā must leave *today*?

PRIYAṂVADĀ. My dear, we shall get over our sorrow. The main thing is that the darling girl should be happy!

ANASŪYĀ. Well then, if you go and fetch that garland of everlasting mimosa I put up for just this occasion—it's in that coconut-shell box, hanging from the branch of the mango—I'll prepare an auspicious paste with deer musk, holy powdered earth, and shoots of sacred grass.

PRIYAṂVADĀ. Let's be about it then!

[ANASŪYĀ *exits.* PRIYAṂVADĀ *deals with the flowers*

OFF-STAGE VOICE. Gautamī, Śārṅgarava, and some others have been appointed to escort Śakuntalā.

PRIYAṂVADĀ [*listening*]. Hurry up, Anasūyā! They've already called up the ascetics who are to go to Hastināpura.*

ANASŪYĀ [*entering with the paste*]. I'm ready! Let's go!

[*They walk about*

PRIYAṂVADĀ [*looking*]. Look, there's Śakuntalā, I can see her newly washed hair gleaming in the risen sun. And now the hermit women are showering her in wild rice and blessings. Let's join them.

[*They approach*

ŚAKUNTALĀ *appears with* GAUTAMĪ *and the* HERMIT WOMEN, *as described.*

FIRST HERMIT WOMAN [*to* ŚAKUNTALĀ]. Child, may your husband grant you the title 'Great Queen',* as a sign of respect!

SECOND HERMIT WOMAN. Child, may you give birth to a great hero!

THIRD HERMIT WOMAN. Child, may you be revered by your lord!

PRIYAṂVADĀ AND ANASŪYĀ [*approaching*]. Dearest, may you be immersed in joy!

ŚAKUNTALĀ. Welcome, my dear friends. Sit down by me.

PRIYAṂVADĀ AND ANASŪYĀ [*sitting*]. Then hold still, darling, while we bless your body with this paste.

ŚAKUNTALĀ. I must make the most of everything now—this too. For when shall my friends make me up in such a way again?

[*She weeps*

PRIYAṂVADĀ AND ANASŪYĀ. Darling—no tears. This should be a happy time.

[*Wiping away her tears, they adorn her using dance movements*

PRIYAṂVADĀ. Your beauty deserves real jewellery—the trinkets lying about the ashram can't do it justice.

Enter two young ASCETICS *carrying something.*

ASCETICS. Here are the very jewels you need—fit for a queen.

[*Everyone stares at them, amazed*

GAUTAMĪ. Nārada, my son, where did these come from?

FIRST ASCETIC. Father Kaṇva's power.

GAUTAMĪ. His mental power?*

SECOND ASCETIC. Not at all. Listen to this! His Holiness had ordered us to bring blossoms from the forest trees for Śakuntalā, but when we went there,

It was a tree itself spun this moon-white cloth, (5)
And a tree that oozed lac to redden her feet,
And gods of the trees that conjured these jewels,
Hands sprouting from branches like fresh green shoots.

PRIYAṂVADĀ [*looking at* ŚAKUNTALĀ]. My dear, this is a sure sign that a royal fortune awaits you in your husband's house.

[ŚAKUNTALĀ *looks modest*

FIRST ASCETIC. Gautamī, come with me. Father Kaṇva's back from bathing now.* Let's tell him about this service the trees have performed.

SECOND ASCETIC. Yes, I'll come with you.

[*Both exit*

PRIYAṂVADĀ AND ANASŪYĀ. We've never worn such ornaments in our lives, but we'll try to arrange them as we've seen it done in paintings.

ŚAKUNTALĀ. I know just how skilful you really are.

[*Dancing, they decorate her*

Enter KAṆVA, *fresh from his bath.*

KAṆVA.

Śakuntalā must leave today— (6)
My sight grows dark with what may come,
My throat is choked, my heart contracts,
A hard ascetic cracked by love.
Then what must worldly fathers feel,
A child departing in this way?
Śakuntalā must leave today.*

[*He walks around*

PRIYAṂVADĀ AND ANASŪYĀ. Dear Śakuntalā, I think we've got your jewellery right. Now let's try this silk, doubled up.

[ŚAKUNTALĀ *rises and puts it on*

GAUTAMĪ. Child, here is your father, filled with tears of joy. I can read in his eyes that he's dying to embrace you. Greet him in the proper way!

ŚAKUNTALĀ [*modestly*]. Father, let me welcome you!

KAṆVA. My dear,

To your lord, may you be (7)
As Śarmiṣṭhā to Yayāti—*
As she bore him Puru, may you bear
Your king a worthy heir.

GAUTAMĪ. Sir, you grant her more than a wish—it's a gift in itself.

KAṆVA. Child, come here and walk around the fires in which the offering has just been made.

[*All walk around*, KAṆVA *chanting a prayer in the Vedic metre**

May these fires ranged around the altar, (8)
Fed by sacred fuel, strewn with darbha,
Dispersing evil through the pungent odour
Of sacrificial offerings, make you pure.

You must set out now! [*Looking around*] Where are Śārṅgarava and the others?

PUPIL [*entering*]. We are here, sir!

KAṆVA. You must show your sister the way.

ŚĀRṄGARAVA. This way, then, sister.

[*They walk around*

KAṆVA. Listen to me, you trees that grow about our hermit's grove.

That girl (9)
who would never let a drop of water
Mist her lips
until she'd watered you,
Who loved you so
she never made a necklace or a bangle from your leaves—
For whom each blossom was the first
and always new,
Must leave the forest for a husband's home today.
And so, for everything Śakuntalā
Has been to you,
give her your blessing now.

[*Miming that he has heard a cuckoo*

Ah, through the cuckoo's song the trees respond— (10)
The departure of Śakuntalā, their forest friend,
Is blessed.

VOICE IN THE AIR.

May her path be charmed by lotus-coloured lakes, (11)
May trees grow shadows in the midday heat,
May the dust of the road be pollen
Beneath her feet, and the breeze blow auspiciously
For Śakuntalā's sake.

[*All hear it with astonishment*

GAUTAMĪ. Child, the goddesses of the grove, who love you like family, have blessed your departure. Let us bow to them now.

ŚAKUNTALĀ [*bowing and turning aside*]. Priyaṃvadā darling, I long to see my noble husband, yet now I have to leave the ashram, my feet are leaden with sorrow.

PRIYAṂVADĀ. You're not the only one to grieve. The grove itself forsees its loss, and suffers with you.

Deer drop their cud, (12)
Peacocks stall their dance,
Leaves fall like tears,
Blanched.

ŚAKUNTALĀ [*remembering*]. Father, I must bid farewell to my sister the vine, to Light of the Forest.

KAṆVA. I know very well how you love her. And here she is.

ŚAKUNTALĀ [*approaching and embracing the vine*]. Light of the Forest, even though you've wound the mango in your branching arms, turn and embrace me in return. After today I shall be far beyond your reach.

KAṆVA.

By your own merits you've attracted (13)
The very husband I'd have wished,
And now the jasmine and the mango
Have entwined, I have no worries left.

This is where your journey starts.

ŚAKUNTALĀ [*to her two friends*]. I leave her in your hands.

PRIYAṂVADĀ AND ANASŪYĀ. But into whose care will you give us?

[*They wipe away tears*

KAṆVA. Don't you weep, Anasūyā—it's up to you to give Śakuntalā strength.

[*They all walk around*

ŚAKUNTALĀ. Father, do you remember that pregnant doe which has been grazing close to the hut because she's so tired from carrying her little one? When she is safely delivered, send someone to tell me the happy news.

KAṆVA. I shall not forget.

ŚAKUNTALĀ [*showing some impediment to her movement*]. Who is pulling at my skirt?

[*She turns around*

KAṆVA. Child:

> That fawn who, when his mouth was spiked by kusha,* (14)
> You healed with oil, and fed with grains of rice
> As though he were your son, and you his mother,
> Refuses now to quit the path.

ŚAKUNTALĀ. Little one, why do you follow me when I'm leaving all my companions? It's true—you were orphaned soon after birth, and I reared you by hand. But now I must leave you too. Father will care for you. Go back!

[*Weeping, she starts to go*

KAṆVA. Have strength!

> Hold back the tears (15)
> That gum your lashes to your eyes,
> Or blind to how the road ahead may rise
> And fall, you'll stumble.

ŚĀRṄGARAVA. Sir, we've reached the shore of the lake, and according to scripture you should accompany those you love no further than the water's edge. So tell us your orders now, and then you can return.

KAṆVA. Let's rest a while first, in the shade of this fig tree.

[*All walk around, then stop.* KAṆVA *speaks to himself*

What would be an appropriate message to send King Duṣyanta?

[*He becomes lost in thought*

ŚAKUNTALĀ [*aside*]. Anasūyā, mark that! How the wild goose honks in anguish because her mate is hidden by lotus leaves . . . But my suffering is worse.

ANASŪYĀ. Don't say that, my dear!

Though the night seems everlasting (16)
Without her mate,*
Hope lifts her—time burns,
And she'll endure the weight
Of separation.

ŚĀRṄGARAVA. Command me, sir.

KAṆVA.

'Consider carefully. We are rich in self-restraint, (17)
Your line is royal; she loved you of her own volition
Without her family's mediation—
So take her as an equal to your other wives.
More, a bride's kinsman can't petition—
The rest is fate.'

ŚĀRṄGARAVA. I have the gist of it.

KAṆVA. Child, now let me give you some advice. You may think I have lived in the forest forever, but I also know the ways of the world . . .

ŚĀRṄGARAVA. A wise man can deal with anything.

KAṆVA. Once you've joined your husband's household:

Be of service to your elders, friendly to his other wives; (18)
Even if your lord offends you, suppress your anger—
don't oppose him;
Be scrupulous with servants, modest in your fortune;
And so become a proper wife
Of whom your family can be proud.

But what does Gautamī think?

GAUTAMĪ. I think you've covered everything a young wife needs to know. Take it to heart, child.

KAṆVA. Now, my dear, embrace me first, and then your friends.

ŚAKUNTALĀ. Father, why must both my dear friends turn back here?

KAṆVA. Dear girl, it won't do for them to accompany you now. They too will be married when the time comes. But Gautamī shall go with you.

ŚAKUNTALĀ [*embracing her father*]. How shall I survive in foreign soil, now that, like a sandalwood vine, uprooted from a mountain slope, I've been torn from my father's side?

KAṆVA. My dear, what is there to fear?

When, as the mistress of your husband's house, (19)
You lose yourself in state affairs,
And when you're mother to a princely son,
Quickened as the sun itself in the eastern sky,
This separation's grief shall fade.

[ŚAKUNTALĀ *falls at her father's feet*

KAṆVA. May everything I wish for you come true!

ŚAKUNTALĀ [*approaching her two friends*]. My dear friends, hug me both at once.

PRIYAṂVADĀ AND ANASŪYĀ [*embracing her*]. Darling, if the king seems slow to recognize you, you must show him the ring he gave you, engraved with his own name.

ŚAKUNTALĀ. Now you make me tremble with your doubts.

PRIYAMVADĀ AND ANASŪYĀ. Don't be afraid! Great love conjures up imaginary evils.

ŚĀRṄGARAVA. The women must hurry now, it is past midday already.

ŚAKUNTALĀ [*turning to face the ashram*]. Father, shall I ever see these ascetic groves again?

KAṆVA. Listen:

> When you have been for many years a queen, (20)
> Co-regent with the sea-engirdled earth,
> And raised Duṣyanta's boy, a champion without peer,
> Your husband shall entrust the kingdom
> To his son and heir, give up his burden,
> And return with you to this green calm.

GAUTAMĪ. Child, the time for us to leave has passed. Release your father now . . . She'll go on saying the same things forever, if you let her, sir. Please turn back now.

KAṆVA. My dear, I've neglected my practice for long enough.

ŚAKUNTALĀ [*embracing her father again*]. This body has been wasted already by ascetic practices. Don't make it worse by too much grieving over me!

KAṆVA [*sighing*].

> Child, when I see that the grains of rice you offered (21)
> Have sprouted in your shelter's doorway,
> How shall grief not overwhelm me?

Go, and may God himself protect you!

[*Exit* ŚAKUNTALĀ *with her escort*

PRIYAMVADĀ AND ANASŪYĀ [*gazing after her*]. Alas! Alas! Śakuntalā has faded into the trees of the forest!

KAṆVA [*with a sigh*]. Anasūyā, your companion has gone—as she had to. So control your sorrow, and follow me home.

PRIYAMVADĀ AND ANASŪYĀ. Father, the ascetic grove is empty without Śakuntalā. How can we ever enter there again?

KAṆVA. The strength of your love makes it *seem* so. [*Walking around, meditatively*] Yes, I am satisfied now that I've seen Śakuntalā off to her husband's house. For:

A daughter's never really ours— (22)
And now I've sent her to her husband's home,
I feel that inner calm a debtor feels
When he's repaid a loan.

[*All exit*

ACT 5

The KING *and the* VIDŪṢAKA *enter and sit down together.*

VIDŪṢAKA. Listen, my friend! Can you hear that melody, so sweet, so clear? It's coming from the music room. If I'm not mistaken, it's the lady Haṃsapadikā, practising a song.

KING. If you'd care to be quiet, I might have a chance of hearing her.

VOICE [*singing in the air*].

Have you forgotten—forgotten so soon, (1)
How you settled on the mango bloom,
Turning nectar to honey with kisses?
Have you really forgotten what bliss is?
To change it so quickly
For the wan and sickly
Night-flowering lotus?

KING. Ah, the melodic line is full of passion.

VIDŪṢAKA. Yes, but did you understand the words?

KING [*smiling*]. I made love to her once. And now she chides me because of Queen Vasumatī.* Friend Mādhavya, tell Haṃsapadikā—using *my* words only, mind—that I have been 'soundly reproached'.

VIDŪṢAKA. As you wish, my lord. [*Rising*] But farewell to liberation! When she grabs my tuft of hair,* I'll be like some passionless ascetic yanked out of his meditation by a heavenly nymph.

KING. Go on! I'm sure a man of your urbanity will have no trouble charming her.

VIDŪṢAKA. What a way to go!

[*Exit* VIDŪṢAKA

KING [*to himself*]. Why should this song fill me with desire, when

I'm not even separated from someone I love? But perhaps

It's what survives of love from other lives, (2)
Trapped in certain forms and sounds,
And then released by song,
That keys my mood
From happiness to longing.

[*He remains in some bewilderment*

The CHAMBERLAIN *enters.*

CHAMBERLAIN. Ah, I'm in a poor way!

This staff I carried like a straw— (3)
Mere badge of office in the king's harem—
Must help me, now my youth's a dream,
To cross a level floor.

A king can't put off his duty. He may have hardly risen from his judgement-seat—and I don't like disturbing him again—but there are these pupils of Kaṇva who have just arrived. There's no rest for those who rule the earth:

Once yoked, the sun must run its course, (4)
The wind must blow both day and night,
The cosmic snake must bear the weight
Of the wide world—and kings perforce
Are bound to nurture and protect
The men they tax.

So I must do my duty too. [*Walking and looking about*] Here's His Majesty:

Like the bull elephant that leads its herd (5)
Through the midday heat, then halts beneath a tree,
This lord is wearied by the constant care
His subjects need, and seeks a place to rest.

[*Approaching*

Victory! Victory to Your Majesty! Some forest ascetics have arrived from the foothills of the Himālayas with a message from sage Kaṇva. They've brought women with them, too. Now Your Majesty will have to work it all out.

KING [*surprised*]. They're messengers? From Kaṇva?

CHAMBERLAIN. They are indeed.

KING. In that case, please tell preceptor Somarāta that he should welcome these hermitage-dwellers with the proper Vedic rites, and then bring them to me himself. I'll be just over there—an appropriate place to greet ascetics.

CHAMBERLAIN. As Your Majesty commands.

[CHAMBERLAIN *exits*

KING [*rising*]. Vetravatī, lead the way to the fire sanctuary.

DOORKEEPER. This way, my lord.

KING [*walking about, showing weariness*]. All beings are happy once they've gratified their desires, except for kings, who must be satisfied with dissatisfaction, for:

Absolute power corrodes itself, (6)
Just maintaining the realm exhausts,
The royal parasol fatigues
Without support.

TWO BARDS [*off-stage*]. Victory to Your Majesty!

FIRST BARD.

Day in, day out (7)
Your own delight
Is subject to the peoples' needs—
Great trees deflect the midday heat
From those who seek their shade.

SECOND BARD.

The miscreant bows before your rod, (8)
You arbitrate and give protection.
Riches and power attract
Spurious relations,
Yet all your subjects,
High or low,
You treat as kinsmen.

KING. How can I feel depressed after that? [*He walks around*

DOORKEEPER. Here's the terrace of the fire sanctuary, fresh from a wash, and there's the cow waiting to give milk for the oblation. Will you step up, Your Majesty?

[*The* KING *ascends, and stands there, leaning on the* DOORKEEPER

KING. Why do you suppose the holy Kaṇva has sent these sages to see me?

Has their practice been disrupted—obstructed? (9)
Has someone threatened the deer—the sacred grove?
Is it something that I've done, or something I've neglected,
Withers their flowering vine?
Vetravatī, don't ask me why—I can't define it—
But this fills me with unease.

DOORKEEPER. I should think that these sages are simply overjoyed by Your Majesty's impeccable conduct, and have come to honour you.

Led by the CHAMBERLAIN *and the* COURT PRIEST, *the* ASCETICS (ŚĀRṄGARAVA *and* ŚĀRADVATA) *enter, with* GAUTAMĪ *and* ŚAKUNTALĀ *in front.*

CHAMBERLAIN. This is the way, sirs!

ŚĀRṄGARAVA. Śāradvata,

I know that this famous king is righteous, (10)
And that even the lowest here are good
[In their peculiar way]; but, to one so long
Secluded, this palace and its people
Burn in hell.

ŚĀRADVATA. How are we supposed to feel in such a place? Look at these city people,

These pleasure-lovers: (11)
I feel like a man fresh from the bath
Caught in a filthy beggar's gaze—*
Pure among the polluted,
Awake among sleepers,
At liberty with slaves.

ŚAKUNTALĀ [*showing that she feels an evil omen*]. Ah, why does my right eyelid tremble so?*

GAUTAMĪ. My child—may every evil be averted, and your husband's family gods grant you happiness!

[*She turns around*

COURT PRIEST [*pointing out the* KING]. There you are, ascetics. The guardian of the sacred and social orders has left the seat of justice and is already awaiting you. Look!

ŚĀRṄGARAVA. It's commendable, of course, but should we be impressed, great priest?

Trees stoop down (12)
with ripening fruit,
Clouds scud the ground
filled with rain,
Great men are civil
with their wealth—
It's their nature
and they go with the grain.

DOORKEEPER. The sages look calm, Majesty. I'm sure they come on peaceful business.

KING [*seeing* ŚAKUNTALĀ]. And the lady?

Who is she, this veiled creature, (13)
Her beauty almost buried,
Surrounded by ascetics
Like a bud by withered leaves?

DOORKEEPER. Majesty, I too am baffled but curious. Perhaps she merits closer inspection?

KING. Enough. One shouldn't stare at another man's wife.

ŚAKUNTALĀ [*with her hand on her bosom, she speaks to herself*]. Why is my heart fluttering? I know my husband's love, so I should be calm.

COURT PRIEST [*going forward*]. Here are the ascetics. They have been duly honoured, and now, if Your Majesty is pleased to hear it, they bring you a message from their preceptor.

KING. I am all attention.

ASCETICS [*raising their hands in greeting*]. May victory be yours, great king!

KING. I salute you all!

ASCETICS. May you fulfil your desires!

KING. Are you able to practise your austerities freely?

ASCETICS.

What could impede the rites (14)
Of the holy men whom *you* protect?
When the sun shines, the dark is checked.

KING. Indeed, my royal title has some meaning now. Does the world benefit from Father Kaṇva's health?

ŚĀRṄGARAVA. Those who have acquired powers control their own health. He asks about yours, and then says this . . . *

KING. . . . I'm his to command.

ŚĀRṄGARAVA. 'You and this daughter of mine married in secret. But that doesn't displease me, and you have my approval.

'We remember you as a man of the utmost honour— (15)
Śakuntalā is virtue itself.
Little wonder the creator brought you together,
A couple so perfectly matched.

'And now that she bears your child, receive her, and perform your duties together as a couple should.'

GAUTAMĪ. Sir, there's something I'd like to say—yet perhaps it's all superfluous:

She ignored her elders, (16)
You never asked her kinsmen.
But you consented to each other . . .
So what can I, or anyone, add to that?

ŚAKUNTALĀ [*to herself*]. What will my noble husband say now?

KING. What is being proposed?

ŚAKUNTALĀ [*to herself*]. The proposal is perfectly clear.

ŚĀRṄGARAVA. 'What is being proposed?' Your Highness is, I suppose, familiar with the ways of the world:

A married woman with her kinsmen's family? (17)
No matter that she's chaste,
People still think the worst.
Cherished or cursed,
She should live with her husband.*

KING. You're saying this lady is already married to me?

ŚAKUNTALĀ [*despondent, to herself*]. My heart knew what was coming!

ŚĀRṄGARAVA.

Is what you've done (18a)
So repugnant now
It swallows your duty?
Or don't you care?

KING. You have no reason to insult me.

ŚĀRṄGARAVA.

This is the magic (18b)
That power works
On moral scruples.

KING. Now you go beyond the bounds.

GAUTAMĪ. Child, put your modesty aside for a moment. Let me lift your veil, and then your husband will know you.

[*She does so*

KING [*staring at* ŚAKUNTALĀ; *to himself*].

They offer me this flawless girl . . . (19)
Could I have married her? I no longer know.
Like a bee mithering at dawn

Round a jasmine soaked in dew,
I can neither approach her, nor go.

[*He remains thinking*

DOORKEEPER [*to herself*]. Ah, duty always comes first for my lord. Who else would hesitate, faced with such a free and beautiful offer?

ŚĀRṄGARAVA. So, king, why do you remain silent?

KING. Ascetics, however hard I try, I don't remember marrying this lady. So how can I accept her when she's obviously pregnant, and I have no reason to believe it's anything to do with me?

ŚAKUNTALĀ [*aside*]. So my lord casts doubt on our very marriage. Where are my high hopes now?

ŚĀRṄGARAVA. No, don't accept her.

Why not insult the sage (20)
Who pardoned the daughter you seduced—
The sage who has made you a gift
Of what you had previously stolen?

ŚĀRADVATA. Śārṅgarava! That's enough! Śakuntalā, we've said what we had to, and the king has given his answer. Now it's up to you to convince him.

ŚAKUNTALĀ [*aside*]. What's the use in reminding him, when passion can change so monstrously? But I owe it to myself to clear my name. [*Aloud*] Dear husband—[*she breaks off in the middle*]—no, my right to address you in that way has been cast into doubt. Puru King, then . . . It becomes you very well to disown a naive and innocent girl with meagre words, after you used them so richly to deceive me in the hermitage.

KING [*covering his ears*]. Enough of this wickedness!

What are you doing? (21)
Like a torrent in spate,
Dissolving its banks,
Undercutting great trees,

You pollute yourself and your family's name
In your vile attempt to shame
And drag me down.

ŚAKUNTALĀ. Very well! If you really think you're in danger of taking another man's wife, let me show you something that will refresh your memory.

KING. An excellent idea.

ŚAKUNTALĀ [*feeling her ring-finger*]. No! It can't be! The ring has gone from my finger!

[*She looks at* GAUTAMĪ, *in despair*

GAUTAMĪ. It must have fallen off when you were bathing at Indra's crossing in the Goddess's holy waters.

KING [*smiling*]. What a nice example of women's proverbial quick-thinking.

ŚAKUNTALĀ. Fate may have taken a hand here, but I have something else to tell you.

KING. Now it's a matter of *hearing* something.

ŚAKUNTALĀ. One day in the jasmine bower, you had in your hand a lotus-leaf cup, full of water . . .

KING. I'm listening.

ŚAKUNTALĀ. Just then, the little fawn—my adopted son, 'Almond Eyes'—appeared, and, feeling kind, you tried to tempt him to sip from the cup. He, being shy of strangers, would not take the water from your hand. But later, when *I* held the cup, he was happy enough to drink. At which, you laughed, and said: 'Everyone trusts their own scent: you are both forest creatures.'

KING. These are the kinds of lying, honeyed words that women use, for their own ends, to lure over-excited youths.

GAUTAMĪ. Great king, you shouldn't speak like that. This girl was brought up in a hermitage; she hasn't the slightest inkling of deceit.

KING. Old woman:

Cuckoos get other birds to raise their chicks (22)
And teach them flight. Females of every kind
Have natural cunning to perform these tricks,
But women, in addition, have devious minds.

ŚAKUNTALĀ [*angrily*]. Wicked man! You see everything through the distorted lens of your own heart. Who else would stoop so low? You cover yourself in virtue like a derelict well, overgrown with weeds.

KING [*to himself*]. Her anger seems real. It almost makes me doubt myself.

When I wouldn't admit to a private affair, (23)
Because I couldn't—and cannot—remember,
Her incandescent eyes and knitted brows
Seemed to break Love's bow,
And reduce it to embers.

[*Aloud*] Lady, Duṣyanta's conduct is open for all to see—and no one sees this in it.

ŚAKUNTALĀ. Yes, I deserve it—I deserve to be called a self-willed wanton, since I put my trust in the Puru dynasty, and gave myself to a man with honey in his mouth but poison in his heart!

[*She covers her face with the hem of her veil and weeps*

ŚĀRṄGARAVA. These impulsive actions always end in pain:

It was all too easy (24)
To contract a secret union
And not divine your lover's true intention,
Which, as so often, was betrayal.

KING. Why, Sir, when you have nothing but this lady's word to go on, do you continue to make these gross insinuations?

ŚĀRṄGARAVA [*disdainfully*]. I'd forgotten—yours is a world turned upside-down:

Those raised to innocence are full of artifice, (25)
But you can trust the liars,—they've put in the practice.

KING. Suppose we allow what you say, Sir Truthteller. Nevertheless, what do you suppose I have to gain by deceiving this woman?

ŚĀRṄGARAVA. Ruin!

KING. Ruin? It's difficult to believe that the Pauravas want to engineer their own downfall.

ŚĀRADVATA. Śārṅgarava, you're wasting your breath. We've carried out our teacher's instructions, and now it's time to go. [*To the* KING]

Here's your wife—take her. (26)
Or forsake her, as you see fit—
A husband's power is absolute.

Gautamī, lead the way.

ŚAKUNTALĀ. What? Have I been deceived by this fraud, for you to abandon me too?

[*She tries to follow them*

GAUTAMĪ [*stopping*]. Śārṅgarava my son, Śakuntalā is following us, crying pitifully. What will my child do, now that her husband has rejected her so cruelly?

ŚĀRṄGARAVA [*turning back angrily*]. Presumptuous girl! What do you want? Independence?

[ŚAKUNTALĀ *trembles, frightened*

Suppose you are no better (27)
Than this king claims?
How could you stay
In Father Kaṇva's house?
But if, as you say,
Your actions leave no stain,
Knowing the truth,
You can bear slavery
At your husband's hearth.

Stay there! We're going without you.

KING. Ascetic, why do you give the lady false hopes?

Nightflowers open for the moon alone, (28)
Sunflowers for the sun:

No one self-restrained would touch
A woman contracted to another man.

ŚĀRṄGARAVA. If you're able to forget a previous affair because of some new attachment, why worry about doing the wrong thing now?

KING [*to the* COURT PRIEST]. You advise me:

Since I no longer know (29)
If I'm deluded
Or this girl's lying,
Tell me which is worse:
Colluding in the ruin of my faithful spouse,
Or risking the defilement
Of another man's wife?

COURT PRIEST [*deliberating*]. Well, in these kinds of cases . . .

KING. . . . What, priest?

COURT PRIEST. Let the lady stay in my house until she gives birth. There's a good reason for that: holy men have already predicted that your first son will bear the bodily signs of a Universal Emperor.* If that turns out to be true of the sage's grandson, then congratulate his mother and receive her into your royal apartments. Otherwise, all you can do is send her back to her father.

KING. As the teacher instructs, then!

COURT PRIEST. Child, follow me.

ŚAKUNTALĀ. Holy Mother Earth, open up and let me in!

[*Starting to weep*, ŚAKUNTALĀ *exits with the* COURT PRIEST *and the* ASCETICS

[*The* KING *remains deep in thought, but he is still unable to remember anything because of the curse*

OFF-STAGE VOICE. Amazing! Quite amazing!

KING [*listening*]. What's happened now?

COURT PRIEST [*coming back in amazement*]. Sir, something truly astonishing has occurred!

KING. Yes?

COURT PRIEST. As soon as Kaṇva's pupils had left,

> The girl threw up her arms and began to cry, (30)
> Lamenting her misfortunes, when—

KING. What?

COURT PRIEST.

> Close to the nymph's shrine, a curtain of light
> Shaped like a woman, whisked her away.

[All are amazed

KING. We've settled the matter already. There's nothing more to say. Your Reverence should get some rest.

COURT PRIEST [*looking at the* KING]. May you be victorious.

[Exits

KING. Vetravatī, I am utterly bewildered. Lead the way to my chamber.

DOORKEEPER. This way, my lord.

[She begins to leave

KING.

> Was she ever really my wife and lover, (31)
> This sage's abandoned daughter?
> I don't remember.
> But my heart's so full of anguish,
> I almost think it may be true.
> Have I betrayed her?

[All exit

ACT 6

The king's brother-in-law, who is the CITY POLICE-CHIEF, *enters with* TWO POLICEMEN, *leading a* MAN *whose hands are tied behind his back.*

POLICEMEN [*beating the man*]. Spit it out, thief! Where did you get this ring? Look at the jewels . . . And the king's name's engraved on it, you bastard!

MAN [*showing fear*]. Give over, boys! I'd never do such a thing!

FIRST POLICEMAN. Oh, I *am* sorry. How could I have missed it? You're some great brahmin, and this is a gift from the king.

MAN. Listen, will you? I'm just a poor fisherman, trying to make a living at Indra's Resort . . .

SECOND POLICEMAN. Did we ask about your caste, thief?

CHIEF. Sūcaka, let him tell it in order from the beginning. Don't keep interrupting!

POLICEMEN. Whatever you say, Chief. Speak up!

MAN. I feed my family by fishing, with nets and hooks, and so on . . .

CHIEF. What a pure profession!*

MAN. You shouldn't say that, sir:

> Others may abuse me, (1)
> But this is my duty:
> No one says to the priest:
> 'You're scum—you feel no pity
> For the sacrificed beast.'

CHIEF. Get on with it!

MAN. One day, I was cutting up a carp, and just lying there in its belly was this nice ring. So I was touting it about, looking for a good price—as you would—and the next thing I know I'm arrested. Finish me off or set me free, that's still the truth!

CHIEF. Jānuka, from the raw stench coming off him, I don't doubt he is a fisherman. But we still don't know how he came by this ring. So straight to the palace, I think.

POLICEMEN. Right. Get a move on, pickpocket!

[*They walk around*

CHIEF. Sūcaka, hold this man at the palace gate! I'll give His Majesty a history of the ring, and report back presently.

POLICEMEN. Bring back something good, Chief!

[*The* CHIEF *exits*

FIRST POLICEMAN. Jānuka, the Chief's been gone forever.

SECOND POLICEMAN. Yes, but you don't just walk in on a king—you have to make an appointment.

FIRST POLICEMAN. Jānuka, my hands are itching to tie on this thief's execution garland.

[*He points to the* MAN

MAN. It's not right—you shouldn't talk about killing a man for no reason at all.

SECOND POLICEMAN [*looking*]. Here comes the Chief, with what looks like the king's warrant. It's the vultures for you, mate. You're staring down the jaws of the dog of death,* all right . . .

CHIEF [*entering*]. Sūcaka, release the fisherman! His story about the ring has been corroborated.

FIRST POLICEMAN. Whatever you say, Chief. He walked through the house of death, and straight out on the other side.

[*He frees the* MAN

MAN [*bowing to the* CHIEF]. What do you think of my profession now, Chief Superintendent?

CHIEF. I've been told to give you a sum equal to the ring.

[*He gives the* MAN *money*

MAN [*bowing*]. I'm much obliged to Your Honour.

FIRST POLICEMAN. That's what I call a favour—to be lifted from the impaling stake straight onto the back of an elephant!

SECOND POLICEMAN. So Chief, I guess this ring was very valuable to the king?

CHIEF. No, I don't think it was the value of the stone that concerned him. He's usually so measured, but when he caught sight of the ring he became really agitated for a while. Just as though he'd remembered someone out of the blue—someone he really cared for, perhaps.

FIRST POLICEMAN. You've done the king a real service then, Chief, that's for certain.

SECOND POLICEMAN. And an even better one to this fisher king.

[*He eyes the* MAN *enviously*

MAN. All right boys, half of it's yours—there's more than a few drinks in that.

SECOND POLICEMAN. It's only fair!

CHIEF. You're really such a *noble* fisherman—you could be my best friend. So I think we should head for the wine-shop now, and celebrate our bond with a bottle or two of wine.*

[*All exit*

From the sky, a nymph called SĀNUMATĪ *enters.*

SĀNUMATĪ. Now the pilgrims have finished bathing at the nymph's shrine, and my guardian duties there are done, I can come and see what King Duṣyanta's up to. Menakā's my friend—her daughter is dear to me—and she asked me to help Śakuntalā, herself. [*Looking around*] Why isn't the palace prepared for the spring festival?* Today's the day. A little meditation would reveal everything, but I promised my friend I would see whatever there was to see with my own eyes. So time to make myself invisible and spy on these two pretty gardeners.

[*She descends and stands there waiting*

A female GARDENER *enters, looking at a mango blossom,* ANOTHER GIRL *following.*

FIRST GARDENER.

Mango, (2)
Your pale bud
Is flushed with pink.
What better reason
To greet you
At the brink
Of the season?

SECOND GARDENER. What are you muttering to yourself, Parabhṛtikā—'Little Cuckoo'?

FIRST GARDENER. 'Little Bee'—Madhukarikā, don't you know the cuckoo becomes unhinged when it sees the mango blossom?

SECOND GARDENER [*rushing over, full of joy*]. Is it the sweet month of Madhu—Spring—already?

FIRST GARDENER. Yes, 'Little Bee', this is the time for your bumbling dances and songs of love.

SECOND GARDENER. Hold me up while I pluck a mango blossom and worship the God of Love.

FIRST GARDENER. Only if half the fruit of your worship is mine.

SECOND GARDENER. You didn't have to ask: we have two bodies but our lives are one. [*She leans on her friend and plucks a blossom*] Ah! Though the blossom's not full-blown, the broken stalk alone has a wonderful scent.

[*She cups her hands together in a gesture of worship*

Mango bud, I offer you to Love: (3)
As he lifts his bow, may he aim you—
The best of his five—*
At deserted young wives,*
Whose husbands roam
Far from native hearth and home.

[*She throws the mango bud into the air*

The CHAMBERLAIN *enters in a fury, tossing the curtain aside.**

CHAMBERLAIN. Not now, you idiotic girl! What do you think you're doing, plucking mango buds, when His Majesty has expressly forbidden all celebration of the spring festival?

BOTH GARDENERS [*frightened*]. Forgive us, sir. We don't know anything about it.

CHAMBERLAIN. What? When even the nesting birds, and the budding trees themselves, obeyed the king's order, you two have heard nothing? Look:

The mango blooms, but sheds no pollen, (4)
The amaranth buds, but will not bloom.
Though winter's gone, the cuckoo's song is frozen,
And Love himself, in his own season, stops
In sudden fear, and lets his arrow drop.

SĀNUMATĪ [*aside*]. This is a powerful king, indeed.

FIRST GARDENER. Sir, we've only been here a few days. We were sent by Mitrāvasu, the king's brother-in-law, to serve the queen. We're newcomers, and nobody told us anything about this. We were just told to look after the pleasure garden.

CHAMBERLAIN. Well, make sure you don't do it again!

BOTH GARDENERS. Sir, we're terribly curious . . . If it's allowed, can you tell us why the spring festival has been cancelled?

SĀNUMATĪ [*aside*]. Mortals love festivals—there must be a pressing reason.

CHAMBERLAIN. I don't see why not. It's common knowledge anyway. Hasn't the scandal of Śakuntalā's rejection reached your ears yet either?

BOTH GARDENERS. The king's brother-in-law told us the ring had been found, but that's all.

CHAMBERLAIN. There's nothing much more to tell. At the sight of the ring, His Majesty remembered that he really had married the Lady Śakuntalā in secret, and then rejected her out of sheer delusion. And ever since, he has been mortified by regret.

Pleasures repel him, (5)
So do affairs of state.

Nights are fitful, sleepless.
For courtesy's sake,
He'll address the palace women,
Only to stall on a name,
Retreat, or go silent with shame.

SĀNUMATĪ [*aside*]. I like the sound of this.

CHAMBERLAIN. In short, the festival's been banned because of the king's depression.

BOTH GARDENERS. It had to be.

VOICE OFF-STAGE. Over here, if it pleases Your Majesty!

CHAMBERLAIN [*listening*]. Ah! The king's coming this way. Go about your business.

BOTH GARDENERS. At once.

[*They exit*

The KING *enters, dressed as a penitent, accompanied by the* VIDŪṢAKA *and the* DOORKEEPER.

CHAMBERLAIN [*observing the* KING]. Whatever the conditions, exceptional beauty always entrances us. Even though wasted with remorse, the king looks wonderful.

Instead of jewels, he wears a single band (6)
Above his left-hand wrist; his lips are cracked
By sighs; brooding all night has drained his eyes
Of lustre; yet, just as grinding reveals
A gem, his austerity lays bare
An inner brilliance and an ideal form.

SĀNUMATĪ [*aside, staring at the* KING]. I can see why Śakuntalā goes on pining for him, even though he rejected and humiliated her.

KING [*pacing about slowly, deep in thought*].

Useless heart—buried in sleep (7)
When my doe-eyed girl
Tried to wake it.
Now it beats in pain

To each pang of remorse,
And shall never sleep again.

SĀNUMATĪ [*aside*]. The poor girl feels exactly the same.

VIDŪṢAKA [*aside*]. Here he goes again—Śakuntalā fever. I don't know how we cure him of that.

CHAMBERLAIN [*approaching*]. Victory to Your Majesty! I have inspected the grounds of the pleasure garden, and it's quite safe for you to go wherever you please, great king.

KING. Vetravatī, take a message to the honourable minister Piśuna—say: 'After a sleepless night, we're not fit to take the judgement-seat today. Please send me a written report of all the civil cases.'

DOORKEEPER. As Your Majesty commands.

[*She exits*

KING. Vātāyana, you too may go on with your work.

CHAMBERLAIN. As the King commands.

[*He exits*

VIDŪṢAKA. Now you've fanned away the flies, take a rest in the garden. It's pleasant enough at this time of day, neither hot nor cold—just right.

KING. My friend, the old saw, 'Misfortune flies into every gap', is all too true:

The dark that gripped recall of Kaṇva's child (8)
Has been dispelled, but straight away, the God
Of Love tips his arrows with mango buds,
And my mind and my soul are fresh impaled.

VIDŪṢAKA. Just wait, and you'll see me break the love god's arrow with my trusty stick.

[*Raising his stick, he tries to break off a mango blossom*

KING [*smiling*]. Let it be! Your brahmin power is overwhelming. So friend, where can I sit and stare at just those particular vines that shall remind me of my love?

VIDŪṢAKA. Didn't you tell your maid, Caturikā, that you would wait in the jasmine bower, and that she should bring you the drawing-board with that portrait of Śakuntalā you painted yourself?

KING. Yes, that's the place to soothe my heart. Take me there now.

VIDŪṢAKA. This is the way.

[*Both walk around;* SĀNUMATĪ *follows*

There's the jasmine bower, welcoming us with offerings of its own flowers. And it wouldn't be complete without a marble bench. So shall we go in and sit?

[*Both enter and sit down*

SĀNUMATĪ [*aside*]. I'll hide behind the creepers,* see the picture of Śakuntalā, gauge the extent of his passion, then tell my friend.

[*She stands behind the creepers*

KING. Friend, now I remember everything. I told *you* about my first meeting with Śakuntalā. I know you weren't there at the time I rejected her, but, when you might have done, you never mentioned her at all. What happened? Did *your* memory go too?

VIDŪṢAKA. No, I didn't forget. You did tell me about it. But you also said it was all untrue—nothing but a joke. And because I'm a dunderhead, I took it at face value. But perhaps there are some things that have to be . . .

SĀNUMATĪ [*aside*]. Many a true word!

KING [*brooding*]. Save me, my friend!

VIDŪṢAKA. What's this? It doesn't suit you. Gales don't shake mountains, and the noblest men are never overwhelmed by grief.

KING. My friend, I'm utterly defenceless against a memory—my love's bewilderment and pain when I denied her:

> Rejected, she followed her kinsmen (9)
> Until Kaṇva's pupil shouted 'Stay!'
> Ah, the look she hurled me then,
> Through tears primed by my cruelty,
> Has turned to a poison
> That works on me still.

SĀNUMATĪ [*aside*]. Such devotion to his own duty! I rejoice in his pain.

VIDŪṢAKA. My guess is her ladyship was carried off by some celestial being . . .

KING. Who else would dare to touch a faithful wife? I have heard that Menakā's her mother. And I feel in my heart it was Menakā's companions who carried her away.

SĀNUMATĪ [*aside*]. It's not his coming to his senses that's astonishing, it's his losing them in the first place.

VIDŪṢAKA. If that's so, then you will certainly meet her again before long.

KING. Why should that happen?

VIDŪṢAKA. No parent can bear to see their daughter parted from her husband for long.

KING.

What was it? Dream? Hallucination? (10)
Vision? The sudden fruition
Of all my good actions at once?*
No matter: I know now
That it's shattered forever,
And like earth in a river
All my fine hopes dispersed.

VIDŪṢAKA. Don't say that. Isn't the ring itself proof that coincidence fashions what has to be?

KING [*looking at the ring*]. I grieve for its expulsion from heaven:

Ring, if your reward (11)
  is anything to go by
Your good deeds
  are as evanescent as mine,
For though you earned a place
  on her matchless, translucent fingers,
You lacked the merit to stick there
  and you fell.

SĀNUMATĪ [*aside*]. If it had fallen into some other hands, that might have been a real reason for grief.

VIDŪṢAKA. As a matter of interest, why did you put the signet ring on her hand in the first place?

SĀNUMATĪ [*aside*]. Yes, I was wondering that as well.

KING. Listen. When I was setting out for the city, my love burst into tears and asked: 'How long will it be before my husband sends news?'

VIDŪṢAKA. Then what?

KING. Then I placed this ring on her finger, and said:

> One by one, day by day, (12)
> Count the syllables
> Inscribed on this ring;
> And when you've spelt my name
> A messenger shall come
> To bring you to the court
> Where you shall be my queen.

But cruelly, I forgot, and no word was ever sent.

SĀNUMATĪ [*aside*]. Such a charming agreement, broken by fate!

VIDŪṢAKA. But how did it get into the carp the fisherman was gutting?

KING. When she was worshipping at Indra's ford, it was carried away by the Ganges's current.

VIDŪṢAKA. It all makes sense now.

SĀNUMATĪ [*aside*]. Yes, I can see that the king might have been afraid his marriage to Śakuntalā, a female ascetic, was doubtful in some way. But a passionate love such as theirs needing a mnemonic? Why was that?

KING. Now, let me castigate this ring.

VIDŪṢAKA [*aside*]. This is the path all madmen take.

KING.

How could you have quit her exquisite finger (13a)
And slipped into that swift and murky river?

Of course,

A mindless ring could never recognize her worth, (13b)
But what about me? Why did I reject my love?

VIDŪṢAKA [*aside*]. Why am I feeling so ravenous?

KING. My darling! Have pity on this mind, giddy with regret. I abandoned you for no reason at all. Let me see you again!

Tossing aside the curtain, CATURIKĀ *enters, carrying the drawing-board.*

CATURIKĀ [*showing the drawing-board*]. Here's the painting you did of the lady.

VIDŪṢAKA [*looking*]. Well done, my friend! You've portrayed your emotion perfectly in the subject-matter—I'm almost stumbling through the hills and hollows just by looking at it.

SĀNUMATĪ [*aside*]. This king's an artist. It's almost as though my friend were standing there before me.

KING.

Her picture's flawed, and she is not— (14)
I lack the art to draw perfection.
But though it's daubed, there is some
Part of her survives its execution.

SĀNUMATĪ [*aside*]. Suffering, it seems, increases modesty as well as love.

VIDŪṢAKA. Now, let me see. Three ladies, and all of them beautiful . . . Which of these, I wonder, can be Śakuntalā?

SĀNUMATĪ [*aside*]. He might as well be blind, if he can't distinguish her beauty!

KING. You guess. Which one?

VIDŪṢAKA. So . . . There's a lady here, standing next to a freshly watered mango-tree, its leaves glistening—her face too from sweat. She's tired, her arms hang limply, her hair's come loose, and some flowers are tumbling from it . . . This, I guess, is Śakuntalā—and the other two her friends.

KING. You're sharp! But perhaps you read the signature of my passion:

Sweat has smeared (15)
the paper where I gripped it;
A tear, from my cheek,
has blistered the paint.

Caturikā, the background's still unfinished. Go and fetch my paints.

CATURIKĀ. Noble Mādhavya, hold the drawing-board until I return.

KING. I shall hold it myself.

[*He takes it. The maid exits*

KING [*sighing*].

I rejected my love (16)
when she stood before me,
Yet now I'm obsessed
by her painted image:
I crossed the stream
of living water
To drink from a mirage.

VIDŪṢAKA [*aside*]. It's too late for the river now, but there's no dispelling the mirage. [*Aloud*] So, my lord, what will you paint here?

SĀNUMATĪ [*aside*]. I should think he'll want to paint those places my friend was so fond of.

KING.

I'll draw the Mālinī, (17)
Flowing through the foothills
Of the great Himālayas,
Its sandbanks a refuge
To browsing deer

And mating geese.
I'll paint
A doe rubbing her eye
On the horn of a black
Antelope buck, beneath
A tree whose branches dip
With the weight of bark dresses,
Hung out to dry.

VIDŪṢAKA [*aside*]. Yes, and soon there'll be nothing in the picture but knot-bearded ascetics.

KING. And another thing, my friend—I've forgotten to draw in any of the ornaments Śakuntalā wore.

VIDŪṢAKA. Such as?

SĀNUMATĪ [*aside*]. Something suited to her forest life and her tender modesty.

KING.

I know—I haven't sketched the mimosa: (18)
Its blossom must be lodged behind her ear,
Its tendrils brush her cheek; and like the autumn
Moon as it spreads its beams, a lotus necklace
Should shimmer on her breast.

VIDŪṢAKA. But why does the lady seem horribly frightened, covering her face with her fingertips, as beautiful and pink as the buds of a pink lotus? [*Looking closely*] Ah, now I see it! That honey-pilfering 'b' of a bee is trying to settle on her face, as though it were a flower.

KING. Impudent insect! Why don't you drive it away?

VIDŪṢAKA. You're the one with power over criminals. You do it!

KING. All right! Why, when every creeper welcomes you, do you waste your time here? Look:

Your thirsty lover waits (19)
On the cusp of a flower—
She won't drink the sweet nectar
Alone.

SĀNUMATĪ [*aside*]. What a polite dismissal!

VIDŪṢAKA. These are the kind that turn nasty when you try to get rid of them.

KING. So you take no notice of me? Listen

Bee, I'm warning you, (20)
I kissed her lips in a rite of passion,
And if you so much as brush them now,
As you might brush a sapling's bud,
A lotus shall be your prison.

VIDŪṢAKA. Such a harsh punishment—why isn't it afraid? [*Laughing, aside*] He's gone mad. And I'll go mad too, if this goes on much longer. [*Aloud*] Because my friend, it's only a bee in a picture.

KING. What picture?

SĀNUMATĪ [*aside*]. I was taken in myself, so I'm not surprised the king couldn't tell the difference.

KING. My friend, what are you trying to do?

She was there in front of me, pure delight— (21)
But now, thanks to you, she's nothing but paint.

[*He sheds a tear*

SĀNUMATĪ [*aside*]. What a contrast between this and how he behaved towards her before!

KING. Friend, why do I suffer this endless pain?

Without sleep, there's no meeting her in dreams, (22)
And even her picture is screened by my tears.

SĀNUMATĪ [*aside*]. I think I can say you've atoned now for that pain your rejection caused Śakuntalā.

CATURIKĀ [*entering*]. Victory to my lord! I was on my way back with the paintbox when . . .

KING. What?

CATURIKĀ. I met Queen Vasumatī and her maid Taralikā on the

path. She snatched the box from my hand, saying: '*I'll* take that to my noble lord!'

VIDŪṢAKA. You did well to get away yourself!

CATURIKĀ. The queen's shawl got snagged in the branches of a tree and, while Taralikā was freeing it, I made my escape.

KING. My friend, the queen is nearby. She's very proud and volatile. You must hide this picture for me.

VIDŪṢAKA. Tell me rather to hide myself. [*Taking the picture and standing up*] If you manage to avoid the traps of the women's apartments, send word to me at the Palace of Clouds.

[*He exits in a hurry*

SĀNUMATĪ [*aside*]. He's still sensitive, it seems, to his first love's feelings,* although his heart's been given to another, and his previous passion dead.

The DOORKEEPER *enters with a message in her hand.*

DOORKEEPER. Victory, victory to the king!

KING. Vetravatī, did you pass the queen on the way?

DOORKEEPER. Indeed, my lord, but she turned back when she saw I had a letter in my hand.

KING. She knows not to interrupt official business.

DOORKEEPER. My lord, the minister requests that you look at this document. He says that the complexity of calculating the various revenues involved has meant that this is the only civil case he has been able to deal with today.

KING. Let me see it.

[*She hands it to him*

[*Reading to himself*] What's this? One of our greatest merchants, Dhanamitra, has been lost at sea . . . and he died without issue, poor man . . . and so, according to the minister, his accumulated wealth goes to me. How terrible to be childless! Vetravatī, this man was rich, and must have had several wives. We should find out if any of them is with child.

DOORKEEPER. My lord, it's said that one of his wives, the daughter of an Ayodhyān merchant, is in her third month, and has performed the ritual to ensure the birth of a son.*

KING. Then the child in the womb inherits by right his father's property. Go and tell the minister!

DOORKEEPER. As the king commands!

[*Starts to go*

KING. Wait a moment!

DOORKEEPER. I'm here.

KING. What does it matter if there's an heir or not?

Announce that, when a man dies, (23)
Untouched by crime,
Duṣyanta will take his place
And guarantee his family
The entire estate.

DOORKEEPER. It shall be proclaimed from the rooftops.

[*Exits, and then re-enters*

The people have received His Majesty's command like timely rain.

KING [*sighing deeply*]. This is how the wealth of families passes to strangers when the last male heir dies without issue. And such will be the fate of the Purus' wealth when I am gone.

DOORKEEPER. God forbid!

KING. I curse myself that I turned my back on my fortune when it came to me.

SĀNUMATĪ [*aside*]. Certainly it is my friend he has in mind when he blames himself.

KING.

I planted the seed of myself, (24)
Then, without lawful reason,
Abandoned my fruitful wife,
Blighting that golden season.

SĀNUMATĪ [*aside*]. Yet your line will not be broken.

CATURIKĀ [*whispering to the* DOORKEEPER]. This story about the merchant has only compounded His Majesty's suffering. Go and fetch noble Mādhavya from the Palace of Clouds to console him.

DOORKEEPER. A good idea!

[*Exits*

KING. Duṣyanta's ancestors are unsettled and ask:

> 'Who will feed us in the afterlife (25)
> As he does now, if there is no heir?'
> And thus distressed, they drink the offering*
> Mixed with tears.

[*He faints*

CATURIKĀ [*looking at him in consternation*]. You'll be all right, my lord! You will be all right!

SĀNUMATĪ [*aside*]. Alas! Alas! The lamp is there, and yet a screen comes between the king and the light, and he is in darkness still. I could make him happy now, but I've overheard great Indra's queen, as she was consoling Śakuntalā, say that the gods themselves, wanting their share of the ancestral offerings, will manoeuvre matters so that her husband will soon greet his lawful wife. So I should wait until the time is fit, and meanwhile console my dearest friend with news of this.

[*She exits into the sky*

VIDŪṢAKA [*off-stage*]. Help! Brahminicide!*

KING [*coming to and listening*]. What? Mādhavya's strangulated voice? Hello! Who's there?

DOORKEEPER [*entering in haste*]. Your friend is in danger, my lord! Please save him!

KING. Who dares to threaten Mādhavya?

DOORKEEPER. An invisible spirit has got hold of him and dragged him onto the roof of the Palace of Clouds.

KING [*rising*]. Don't even say it! In my own household, and not protected from spirits! But then:

How can I keep track (26)
Of my subjects,
When from day to day
I have no idea
Which way I'm going myself?

VIDŪṢAKA [*off-stage*]. Help me, friend! Help me!

KING [*starting to move quickly*]. Don't be afraid!

VIDŪṢAKA [*off-stage, still calling for help*]. Don't be afraid? When something's forcing my neck back and trying to split it in three like a sugarcane stalk?

KING [*looking around*]. My bow! Now!

BOWBEARER [*entering*]. Your bow, arrow, and wrist-guard, my lord.

[*The* KING *takes them*

OFF-STAGE VOICE.

I'll kill you as a tiger (27)
Kills his kicking prey,
And suck the blood,
From your tattered, pulsing throat—
Or let Duṣyanta,
Who claims to meet all threats,
And face down danger with his bow,
Convey you to some place of safety—
If he can.

KING [*angrily*]. You dare to address me so? Stay there, you carrion-eater! Now's your time to die! [*Stringing his bow*] Vetravatī, to the stairs!

DOORKEEPER. This way, my lord!

[*All rush forward in haste*

KING [*looking all around*]. Where are they? It's empty!

VIDŪṢAKA [*off-stage*]. Help! Help! I can see you—can't you see me?

There's no hope for me then—I'm like a mouse in the claws of a cat!

KING. Spirit! You may be invisible, but my arrows have no need of sight! Now I draw my bow, and now:

As a goose siphons milk (28)
From a pool of water,* I'll save
The brahmin, as he deserves,
And deliver you to your well-earned death.

[*He aims his arrow*

Immediately MĀTALI *appears, at the same time releasing the* VIDŪṢAKA.

MĀTALI.

Indra makes demons your target— (29)
Aim your arrows at them.
As for your friends, let
Love be your weapon.

KING [*dropping his aim in haste*]. Aha! It's Mātali! You are welcome, great Indra's charioteer!

VIDŪṢAKA. He tries to kill me like a sacrificial beast, and you welcome him with open arms!

MĀTALI [*smiling*]. Ageless King! Will you hear why Indra has sent me to you?

KING. I am all attention.

MĀTALI. There's a near-invincible brood of demons, descended from Kālanemi . . . *

KING. Yes, Nārada* once told me about them.

MĀTALI.

The sun doesn't touch that night (30)
The moon dispels. To those demons
Indra is the sun, and you the moon—
So you should be the one to fight.

You are armed already, my lord. You only have to mount Indra's chariot, and victory is assured!

KING. Indra honours me, indeed. But why this rough treatment of Mādhavya?

MĀTALI. Quite simple. I saw you were depressed for one reason or another, and sought to rouse you by making you angry.

> Stir the embers and the fire leaps up, (31)
> Threaten the snake and its hood expands—
> Everything in nature, if provoked, responds.

KING [*aside to the* VIDŪṢAKA]. Friend, I cannot ignore the Lord of Heaven's command. Inform Minister Piśuna what's happened, and tell him this from me:

> Concentrate your mind on protecting the realm: (32)
> My bow and I have godly business to perform.

VIDŪṢAKA. Whatever the king commands.

[*Exits*

MĀTALI. To the chariot, great lord!

[*The king mounts the chariot. All exit*

ACT 7

The KING *and* MĀTALI *enter from the direction of heaven, on a flying chariot.*

KING. Mātali, I only did what Indra asked of me. That hardly seems to merit the special treatment I've received.

MĀTALI [*smiling*]. It seems to me you're both unsatisfied, my lord:

Because Indra himself picks you out (1)
For high distinction, you feel surprise,
And think you must be undeserving.
But to him such plaudits seem a meagre prize
For the prince who destroyed such demons.

KING. Not at all, Mātali! As I was leaving, he honoured me beyond any possible expectation, allowing me to share his throne in front of all the gods.

When Jayanta* saw his smiling father (2)
Give me a garland of coral,
Stained by that same heavenly sandal
That decorates great Indra's body,
His envy could hardly be suppressed.

MĀTALI. Ageless Lord, tell me what you don't deserve from the king of the immortals. Consider:

Twice now, Indra's pleasure-heaven has been saved (3)
From spiny demons—once by Viṣṇu
With his man-lion claws,* and then by you
With your streamlined arrows.

KING. But here too, it's the greatness of Indra that should be praised.

However much the man aspires, (4)
Success depends upon his lord's
Commission. Dawn would be trying

To smudge the darkness still,
Had the sun not made him
His charioteer.

MĀTALI. It's an excellent attitude! [*After going further*] Look there, my lord! See how your fame lights up the vault of heaven!

On palm leaves plucked from the wish-giving tree, (5)
With a palette of celestial nymphs' cosmetics,
Your immortality is sanctioned in a sketch,
Or heavenly song.

KING. Mātali, I was so eager to fight demons, I didn't notice the path we took yesterday as we flew into the heavens. But what wind course are we on now?

MĀTALI.

This is the path of the wind, Parivaha,* (6)
Freed from darkness by Viṣṇu's second stride—
The wind that swells the Gaṅgā's triple tide
And buffets light from the orbiting stars.

KING. Mātali, this is why my body, mind, and soul are calm. [*Looking at the chariot wheels*] Now, I think, we're descending to cloud level.

MĀTALI. How do you know that?

KING.

Lightning buffs the horses' coats, (7)
Our wheels glisten from rain and mist;
Cuckoos swerve between their spokes.

MĀTALI. Shortly, we shall come to earth in your very own kingdom, my lord.

KING [*looking down*]. The speed of our descent turns the human realm into something amazing!

Now a mountain peak appears, the world (8)
Seems to flow like lava down its face;
Branches are salvaged from a sea of leaves;
Ribbons turn to rivers; now the earth

Heaves up to meet me, as though some giant hand
Had pushed it into space.

MĀTALI. Well observed! [*Looking down with reverence*] Ah, but the world is beautiful!

KING. Mātali, what mountain range is that, standing between the eastern and western oceans, running it seems with liquid gold, like a cloudbank at sunset?

MĀTALI. It is indeed called 'Golden Peak', the mountain of the demigods, where asceticism ends in perfect success, my lord.

Mārīca, lord of creation, (9)
Sprung from self-existent Brahmā,
Father of gods and demons,*
Leads a life of penance there
With Aditi his wife.

KING. One shouldn't fly past fortune! I shan't go on until I've walked in worship round the holy sage.

MĀTALI. An impeccable resolve!

[*They start to descend*

KING [*astonished*].

The chariot descended (10)
Without seeming to descend—
Without the slightest sound,
Or coil of dust,
Or bridle twitch,
It hovers just above the surface
Of the earth.

MĀTALI. That is the difference between you and Indra, my lord.

KING. Where is Mārīca's hermitage, Mātali?

MĀTALI [*pointing*].

There, where that sage (11)
Is rooted like a tree-trunk,
Staring at the sun,

Buried in an anthill
High as the snake skin
That girdles his chest,
Half-strangled
By the dried and shrinking vine
Entwined around his neck,
His shoulders shrouded
In his matted hair,
Bulging with the nests
Of sweet śakunta birds,
Is where you'll find this lord.

KING. I bow to that sage for his great penance.

MĀTALI [*reining in the horses*]. Now we are entering Mārīca's hermitage, where the coral trees are tended by Aditi herself.

KING. A place more tranquil than heaven! I feel as though I'm floating in a pool of nectar.

MĀTALI [*stopping the chariot*]. You may get down now, my lord.

KING [*alighting*]. And what about you, Mātali?

MĀTALI. I'll secure the chariot and get down too. [*He does so*] This way, sir. [*Turning around*] Up ahead, you can make out the seers' penance groves.

KING. It's an astonishing sight!

In a wood of trees that grant all wishes, (12)
These ascetics live on air. Where they bathe,
The lotus gilds the water with its pollen;
They meditate on marbled, jewel-encrusted stairs,
Dead to the charms of celestial women—
Ascetics in that very heaven
That others through their practice hope to gain.

MĀTALI. The great attempt the greatest ends. [*He walks about, calling aloud*] Ancient Śākalya, what is the venerable Mārīca doing? What do you say? . . . Prompted by Aditi's questioning, he's addressing the seers' spouses about the responsibilities of a devoted wife?*

KING [*listening*]. With such a subject, we must wait our turn.

MĀTALI [*looking at the king*]. Your Majesty could sit at the foot of this ashoka tree, while I find the right moment to announce your arrival to Indra's father.

KING. Whatever you advise.

[*He sits*

MĀTALI. I shall go now.

[*He exits*

KING [*sensing an omen*].

My desire is hopeless, yet this vein (13)
Throbs in my arm—*
Once abandoned, fortune
Is incessant pain.

OFF-STAGE VOICE. Don't act so rashly! How he reverts to his nature!

KING [*listening*]. This is no place for uncontrolled behaviour. Who can they be reprimanding? [*Looking in the direction of the voice, surprised*] Ah! And what kind of child is this, guarded by two female ascetics, and so much stronger than his years? For:

As a game (14)
He's manhandled this cub,*
Dragged its mane
From its mother's dripping dug.

Enter the BOY *as described, accompanied by two female* ASCETICS.

BOY. Lion, open your mouth! I want to count your teeth!

FIRST ASCETIC. Naughty boy! Why do you tease the animals we love like children? You seem to get wilder by the minute. The seers were right to call you 'Sarvadamana'—'All Tamer'!

KING. Why am I drawn to this child, as though to my own son? Precisely because I don't have a child of my own . . . It must be playing on my mind.

SECOND ASCETIC. If you don't let her cub go, the lioness will maul you!

BOY [*grinning*]. Oh, I'm so frightened!

[*Pouting*

KING.

In this child (15)
There's a seed
Of astonishing force;
Like a spark,
It needs nothing but fuel
To break into life.

FIRST ASCETIC. Child, let go of the cub and I'll give you something else to play with!

BOY. Where is it? Give it to me!

[*He stretches out his hand*

KING. How can that be? He bears the marks of a world ruler. For:

Now, as he opens his hand (16)
To grasp some toy,
I see how delicately his palms are webbed,*
Like a lotus, whose petals
Never quite part
In the first faint light of day.

SECOND ASCETIC. Suvratā, words alone won't stop him. Go to my hut and fetch that painted peacock, the toy seer Mārkaṇḍeya's son left behind.

FIRST ASCETIC. I'll get it.

[*She exits*

BOY. But this cub's still my toy while I'm waiting!

[*He looks at the ascetic and laughs*

KING. There's something draws me to this spoilt boy.

Lucky the man who cradles in his lap (17)
His little son, and breathes the dust that mats

His hair, touches the buds of his first milk teeth,
Anticipates his stammering speech.*

SECOND ASCETIC. See how he ignores me! [*She looks back*] Are any of the sages' sons there? [*Seeing the* KING] Sir, please come here! I can't loosen his grip on the little cub. To him it's just a game to torment it!

KING [*approaching with a smile*]. Oh son of a great sage,

You were born to self-restraint, (18)
So why break the rule of the sanctuary,
And like an infant snake in a sandal tree
Disturb such perfect harmony?

SECOND ASCETIC. Good sir, he's no sage's son!

KING. That I should have guessed from his actions and his looks. It was just the surroundings misled me . . .

[*He does as she asks. At the touch of the* BOY, *he speaks to himself*

When I, a stranger, steal a frisson (19)
From this boy's touch,
What can limit his father's joy,
Who watches, day by day,
His son grow up?

SECOND ASCETIC [*looking at them both*]. What an extraordinary thing!

KING. What is it, madam?

SECOND ASCETIC. I'm astonished that you and the boy are so alike! And though he's never seen you before, he's not at all shy.

KING [*fondling the boy*]. If he's no hermit's child, then what's his lineage?

SECOND ASCETIC. He belongs to Puru's family.

KING [*to himself*]. What! We belong to the same lineage? No wonder she thinks we resemble each other. And, indeed, the Puru line does have a family vow:

As world-protectors they begin (20)
In castles crammed with sense delights,

But later make the wood their home
With holy men and anchorites.

[*Aloud*] But mortals don't have the power to enter this place on their own.

SECOND ASCETIC. You're quite right, sir. But because his mother is the daughter of a nymph, she was allowed to give birth to him here in Mārīca's hermitage.

KING [*to himself*]. More ground for hope. [*Aloud*] The lady's husband—what is that royal seer's name?

SECOND ASCETIC. Who would think to pronounce the name of a man who's cast off his lawful wife?

KING [*to himself*]. This may be my story. Now, if I were to ask the name of the boy's mother . . . But then it's not done to ask about some other man's wife.

FIRST ASCETIC [*entering with a clay peacock in her hand*]. Sarvadamana, look at the śakunta landing! What a pretty bird!

BOY [*looking around*]. Mamma? Where is she?*

BOTH ASCETICS. He wants his mother. It was the similar-sounding name that tricked him.

SECOND ASCETIC. Darling, she just wanted you to look at the lovely clay peacock, the śakunta bird.

KING [*to himself*]. What! His mother's name's Śakuntalā? But even that name is not unique, and like a mirage may lead to nothing but despair.

BOY. Auntie, I like this pretty peacock!

[*He takes the toy*

FIRST ASCETIC [*looking about anxiously*]. Ah no, he's lost the amulet that protects him—there's nothing on his wrist!

KING. Don't worry. He dropped it there when he was wrestling with the lion cub.

[*He goes to pick it up*

BOTH ASCETICS. Don't touch it! . . . Ah, too late, he's picked it up!

[*Clasping their hands to their bosoms, they stare at each other in amazement*

KING. Why shouldn't I touch it?

FIRST ASCETIC. Listen, great king. At the time of his birth ritual, lord Mārīca gave him the herb contained in this amulet. It's called Aparājitā, 'The Invincible'. If it's dropped, no one can pick it up—apart from his parents and himself.

KING. And if someone else does take it up?

FIRST ASCETIC. Then it changes into a snake and bites him.

KING. Have you ladies ever seen it change in such a way?

BOTH ASCETICS. Many times.

KING [*delighted, to himself*]. Then let me rejoice, for I have my heart's desire.

[*He embraces the boy*

SECOND ASCETIC. Suvratā, over here. This is news, indeed, with which to interrupt Śakuntalā's austerities.

[*Both exit*

BOY. Let me go! I want to go to Mamma!

KING. My little son, we shall greet your mother together.

BOY. Duṣyanta's my Daddy, not you!

KING [*smiling*]. A denial that makes it certain.

ŚAKUNTALĀ *enters, as though in mourning, with her hair tied in a single braid.**

ŚAKUNTALĀ. They tell me Sarvadamana's amulet didn't change, but why should I believe my fortune has, because of that? Yet perhaps what Sānumatī says is true . . .

KING [*seeing* ŚAKUNTALĀ]. Ah, it *is* the lady Śakuntalā!

Her robes are dusky, drab, (21)
Her hair a single braid,

Her cheeks drawn in by penance—
She's been so pure and constant
In that vow of separation
I so callously began.

ŚAKUNTALĀ [*seeing the* KING *pale from suffering*]. He doesn't look like my husband. Who is this who dares to pollute my son with his touch, in spite of the amulet?

BOY [*running to his mother*]. Mamma, this stranger is calling me his son!

KING. My dear, that cruelty I practised on you has come full circle, since now it is I who need to be recognized by you.

ŚAKUNTALĀ [*to herself*]. Heart, be calm, be consoled. My bitter fate has turned compassionate. It is indeed my husband.

KING. My dear,

Memory breaks my black delusion: (22)
Beautiful as Rohiṇī,*
Back with her lord
After his lunar eclipse,
You stand before me.

ŚAKUNTALĀ. Victory, victory to my noble husb-

[*She breaks off in the middle, her voice choked by tears*

KING. Beautiful lady,

Choked by tears, you couldn't say it, (23)
But the victory *is* mine—
For in looking on your pale
Unpainted lips, I have at last
Recalled your face.

BOY. Mamma, who is he?

ŚAKUNTALĀ. Ask what shares you have in fate, my child.

KING [*falling at* ŚAKUNTALĀ*'s feet*].

Let the pain of my rejection (24)
Pass from your heart.

I was deluded, blocked by the dark
From my own good fortune,
Blind as the man who tore at his neck,
Believing his garland a snake.

ŚAKUNTALĀ. Arise, my husband! I must have done something terrible in a previous life, and was punished for it at just that time.* If not, why would your gentle heart have hardened towards me? [*The* KING *rises*] But how did my lord remember this woman whose portion is pain?

KING. I'll tell you, but first let me pull this barb of sorrow from my heart.

Deluded, I once ignored (25)
A tear that smudged
Your quivering lip.
Now let me wipe away its sister
Trembling on your lash,
And with it my remorse.

[*He does so*

ŚAKUNTALĀ [*seeing the signet ring*]. Noble husband, this is the ring!

KING. And when it was recovered, my memory recovered too.

ŚAKUNTALĀ. It acted unfaithfully—at the very time I needed to convince my husband, it went missing.

KING. Then let the vine take this flower back as a sign of her reunion with spring.

ŚAKUNTALĀ. I don't trust it now. You wear it, my lord.

MĀTALI *enters.*

MĀTALI. Congratulations, my lord! Reunited with your lawful wife, and able to gaze on your little son's face.

KING. My desire has ripened into a sweet fruit. But, tell me Mātali, didn't Indra know all about this?

MĀTALI [*smiling*]. What do such lords not know? Come now, Majesty. Lord Mārīca has granted you an interview.

KING. Śakuntalā, bring our son. I should like the three of us to see Mārīca together.

ŚAKUNTALĀ. I am embarrassed to go before my elders in my husband's company.

KING. But you should, when the occasion is so joyful. Come . . . come.

They all walk around. Then MĀRĪCA *enters with* ADITI, *and they sit*

MĀRĪCA [*seeing the* KING]. Aditi:

This is the world's protector, (26)
King Duṣyanta,
Who leads Indra's armies
To battle.
His bow is the reason
Your son's thunder-
Bolt, and other weapons,
Lie redundant.

ADITI. I could tell as much just by looking at him.

MĀTALI. Majesty, here are the parents of the gods looking at you with a parental eye. You may approach them.

KING. Mātali:

Is this that couple sages say (27)
Sprung from Marīci and Dakṣa,*
The sons of creator Brahmā—
That couple who are themselves
The source of the fiery sun's
Twelve forms*—parents of Indra
Who rules the triple world,
The sacred family into which
Self-existent Viṣṇu,
The universal form,
Consented to be born?

MĀTALI. Even so.

KING [*approaching*]. Duṣyanta, Indra's servant, bows before you.

MĀRĪCA. May you live long, my son, to protect the earth!

ADITI. Be an invincible hero, my son!

ŚAKUNTALĀ. My son and I worship at your feet.

MĀRĪCA. Daughter:

If your husband's (28)
like Indra
And your son
like Jayanta,
Then may you be
like Paulomī—*
That's the only
apt blessing.

ADITI. Daughter, may your husband show you the greatest honour. And may your son live long to the delight of both your families! Now, sit.

[*They all sit down before* MĀRĪCA

MĀRĪCA [*pointing to each in turn*].

Fortune unites faith, wealth, and order: (29)
Śakuntalā the pure, her noble son, the king.

KING. Lord, my deepest wish was granted first, and *then* I saw you—an unprecedented kindness, for:

Causes normally usher in effects— (30)
Clouds bubble up before a downpour,
The flower blossoms first, and then the fruit—
But here, fortune anticipates your favour.

MĀTALI. This is the way creators create blessings.

KING. Sir, I married this lady, your servant, in secret. Later, when her relatives brought her to join me, my memory failed; I rejected her, and sinned against your kinsman, the sage Kaṇva. Later still I saw this ring, and then it came to me that I had indeed married his daughter. It all seems so strange . . .

I am like a man who disbelieves (31)
The evidence of his eyes:
For all its obvious size,
He doubts the elephant exists—
Until there's no elephant, only prints,
And then he's suddenly convinced.
Such was the miasma that poisoned my mind.

MĀRĪCA. My son, you mustn't blame yourself. Even your delusion had due cause. Listen to me . . .

KING. I am all attention.

MĀRĪCA. When Menakā came to Aditi, transporting her daughter from the nymphs' ford in such obvious distress, I saw, in meditation, that you had rejected your forest wife because of a curse, spoken by Durvāsas. I saw too that the curse would lift when you caught sight of this ring.

KING [*sighing with relief*]. So—I am not to blame.

ŚAKUNTALĀ [*to herself*]. It's good to know my husband didn't reject me for no reason at all. And yet I don't remember being cursed. Or perhaps it fell unnoticed through the emptiness of separation that engulfed me then. My friends did urge me to show the ring to my husband.

MĀRĪCA. Daughter, now you know the truth. Feel no resentment towards your lord:

When his memory was cursed, (32)
Your husband was cruel to you,
But that darkness has lifted
And your power's renewed;
The mirror was tarnished,
The image obscure,
But with polishing
It all becomes clear.

KING. Just as Your Holiness says.

MĀRĪCA. My son, I hope you have greeted your little boy, born of Śakuntalā, with due delight. We have initiated him with all the proper rites.

KING. Holiness, the greater glory of my line rests in him.

MĀRĪCA. It does, and you should know, my lord, that he will be a universal emperor,

> Gliding on a chariot cushioned by air (33)
> Across the ocean's rough waters—a warrior
> Who will rule the earth's seven continents
> Without resistance. Here, he's Sarvadamana,
> All-Tamer; later, when he bears the world,
> The world will call him Bharata, Sustainer.*

KING. Since *you* performed his birth rights, lord, we can expect nothing less.

ADITI. Sir, Kaṇva should be told that his daughter's hopes have been fulfilled. Menakā, who loves her daughter so, keeps attendance on us here.

ŚAKUNTALĀ [*to herself*]. Her ladyship's speech and my desire are one.

MĀRĪCA. Through the power of his practice, he knows everything already.

KING. That must be why the sage never turned his anger on me.

MĀRĪCA. Nevertheless, we should tell him of this happy event. Who's there!

PUPIL [*entering*]. I am here, sir.

MĀRĪCA. Gālava, go now by the sky route and tell Kaṇva this happy news from me: Śakuntalā and her son have been recognized by Duṣyanta, now the curse has been broken and his memory restored.

PUPIL. As my lord commands.

[*He exits*

MĀRĪCA. My son, now you must mount your friend Indra's chariot and return to your capital with your wife and boy.

KING. As His Holiness commands.

MĀRĪCA.

May your great sacrifices please (34)
The great god Indra,
And may he please your subjects with rain.
And so let time and seasons pass
In mutual service,
A benefit to both our realms.

KING. Holiness, I shall strive for this with all my power.

MĀRĪCA. My son, what further joy may I bestow?

KING. What greater joys than these? But if Your Holiness wishes to bestow something else, let it be this:

May the king work for the good of nature, (35)
May we honour those versed in revelation,
And may the universal power
Of self-existent Śiva,
Free me from rebirth and death
Forever.*

[*All exit*

ŚAKUNTALĀ IN THE *MAHĀBHĀRATA*

(*Mahābhārata*, 1.62–9)

NOTE: Marginal numbers refer to the verse numbers of the Sanskrit text.

Duṣyanta was a Paurava forefather,* 1.62.3
A hunter through the wide world
To its hidden places,
A lord of lords, whose joy
Was the open earth—its quarters,
Countries, oceanic islands.
To barbarous shores and tribal forests,
To every cliff drubbed by the pearl-gloved sea,
To the Āryan limit*
This king held sway. 5

It was a golden time—
No need to mine, or plough the earth,
No marriage not a proper match,
No evil done or thought.
The people were devotees
Of their own duty
While King Duṣyanta reigned,
Wealth and religion their only aim,
Theft a fiction,
Disease a mirage,
Starvation an improbable dream.

Each to his duty
And each to selfless worship
In this king's care.
No fear at all—rain rained
As it must, crops grew
As they should,
Stones were gems,
Wealth a flood. 10

And the king himself?
A miracle of youth and adamantine strength:
He could have plucked up Mount Mandara,*
Trees, forests, jungles—the lot,
And carried it off like a paper cone.

Pick your weapon—bow, club, or sword,
He was its master on elephant or horseback.
Strong as God, blinding as the sun,
Unruffled as the ocean deep,
Solid as the compacted earth—
Yes, he was well thought of.
From border to border,
From hovel to palace,
The kingdom was peaceful
And the people of one good mind.

Then, in this golden season, 1.63.1
The king rode out with his entourage:
Hundreds of horse and elephant teams,
Swords, lances, javelins,
Clubs, maces, and spears—
Name a weapon, there it was,
Where the clamour of warriors, rank and file,
The braying conches, drums,
The churning chariot wheels,
The trumpeting elephants, whinnying horses,
And the growling, shoulder-slapping men
Filled the street from wall to wall.

But riding above that dust and noise,
High on their balconies,
The palace women craned to glimpse
Their regal hero,
Aureoled in his own fame. 5
To them he was Indra,* an enemy-killer,
A god like a wall to hostile elephants.
'He's a tiger in a man's body,' they cried,
'Ripping up battlefields,
Burying the foe!'
They loved him, those women, sang his praises,
Dropped blossoms round his head
Like showers of summer rain.
(Brahmins praised him too.)

Rippling with joy,
He made for the forest, the chase.
For miles they trailed him, townsman and villager—
Until, with a gesture, he turned them back.
He was lord of the earth,
But it was the sky
That cracked with the sound of his chariot
Like Garuḍa in flight.*

Weaving and swaying he spotted at once
A wooded tract, a paradise,
With fertile groves,
And rolling hills and boulder-punctuated plains,
Terra firma, terra incognita,
Not a human sight or sound.

But that forest was alive—teeming
With deer, their predators, and other game,
And Duṣyanta, a predator himself,
Was even-handed when it came to slaughter—
Tiger families were shredded,
Slashed, shafted, pierced.
Antelopes?—Spear-fodder,
Club-corpses.
Nothing threw or stretched his courage,
Whatever he tried from his armoury—
Javelin, sword, mace, bludgeon, halberd—
The result was the same: dead fowl, dead game.

Bigger beasts saw him coming,
A king riding the wave of his troops.
All too late for the culled, leaderless deer,
Who bleated in vain: for they were exhausted,
The rivers were dust,
Their hearts strained to breaking.
Empty and dry, some crumpled unconscious,
And men of the woods, half-beast themselves,
Consumed them raw where they lay.
Others were spitted to roast,

Cut up and consumed in a civilized way.
Sword-gashed, great elephants ran beserk,
Trunks curled the air, stampeding and frantic,
Shitting and pissing,
Streaming with blood,
Trampling hunters like snails—
Wild, deranged, in a forest
Drenched by a cloudburst of violence,
A storm of power and iron, a royal cull,
Boiling,
Overflowing with buffalo.

Ten thousand dead deer 1.64.1
Were not enough for king and entourage;
They pushed into the wood
In search of better, fitter game.

As famished and as thirsty,
Yet stronger than the rest,
Duṣyanta pressed deeper still,
Coming at last to a secret place
Of scattered shacks and hovels,
A holy corner of the forest world,
That sprung his hunter's heart and soothed his eye.

But even there he would not pause,
Making instead for another wood,
Where a cool breeze
Rippled through blossoming boughs
And smoothed the matted grass—
A cavern of light and air,
Echoing with trills and runs,
Where the quick shadows of birds in flight
Merged with the deeper shadows
Of foliate trees,
Creeper-covered
And surging with bees,
Under the rule and sway
Of beauty.

It was a forest singing to itself,
To its blossoms and thornless fruit,
A performance paid in perpetual blooms,
Garlanding the velvet moss,
And not a tree unblackened by bees.

Stirred by a gentle wind,
Petals like spiralling snow
Descended onto the king.
Trees in their patchwork robes,
Touching the skies,
Stood in welcoming line,
While under their bud-bent boughs
A rug of sound was spread
By bees and birds.

Gazing on vistas of flowers,
On creepers pavilioned in creepers,
The king's delight mounted to joy.
It could have been the festival
Of spring: trunk joined to trunk
In a tracery of their own
Blossoming branches, pollen
Pollinating a breeze
That swept through the trees,
Taking each as its lover—
A wood wrapped in its rivers,
A forest of banners
Crowding the sky.

Birds flew up,
And following their flight,
Through a haze of woodsmoke,
Duṣyanta saw a model hermitage,
Peopled by anchorites,
Ascetics, and other religious types—
The forest floor pitted with their fires.
It was on the flowering banks
Of the holy Mālinī,

Bridging its inlets,
Somewhere between heaven and earth,
A shimmering sanctuary
For wildfowl, deer, and beasts of prey—
A sight that filled the king with joy.

Approaching this earthly paradise,
He saw how, like a mother
To all living things, the holy river's
Veins fed the whole hermitage:
Sheldrake sheltered on her banks,
In her current, blossom and foam
Mixed as one; centaurs, monkeys, bears
Flourished in her fertile care;
Across her ripples came the drone
Of Vedic chant,* taming
Tigers, rutting elephants, great snakes.

What king could resist these woodland depths,
This shimmering river and its graceful banks?
It might have been Nara and Nārāyaṇa's*
Retreat on the shores of the Gaṅgā,
Echoing with the peacock's shriek,
And the hermitage itself
Citraratha's field.*

At the threshold, he thought, 'I'll visit Kaṇva,
That peerless seer and great ascetic,
That paragon whose brilliance blinds description',
And said aloud:

'I shall call on Kaṇva Kāśyapa, dispassionate sage,
Wealthy with penance. Wait for me here!'

His charioteers and bodyguards withdrew.

He might have been in Indra's heaven:*
He felt no hunger there, or thirst,
But ate and drank the woodland's joy.

With ministers and a palace priest,
He went on foot to greet the sage
Who'd built that everlasting penance park,
Retreat of all retreats,
Mirror to the world of Brahmā,*
A-hum with bees and milling birds.

Then in the wind he heard
The drone of priests reciting hymns,
Veda-trained brahmins with their slow-building rituals—
Word by word, verse by verse—
Specialists in truth and revelation,
Pacing their sacrificial enclosures . . .*
And now, wherever he looked,
Self-restrained brahmins,
Mutterers of mantras, offerers of offerings,
Were keeping their vows.
And out of nowhere,
A clearing, full of bright seating,
Cushioned with flowers.

What with this, and so many priests
Making devotions at heavenly altars,
He supposed himself lost
In the world of Brahmā.
But who could tire of that hermitage
Kaṇva's penance protected,
Hallowed by brahmins?

And so this king,
With his ministers and priest,
Set foot in Kaṇva's kingdom of seers,
Crowded yet solitary,
Fertile with penance,
Disarming and holy.

But now it was time to dismiss his companions 1.65.1
And go on alone . . .

The hermitage was deserted,
Or so it seemed
(But then the seer followed a strict regime).
In the surrounding enclosure, nothing moved.
The king called out:
'Is anyone here?'
His voice rippling like thunder
Through the sultry air.

A girl appeared,
Śrī herself,* it seemed, in hermitage rags . . .
Dark eyes.

'Welcome', she said without hesitation,
Honoured him, showed him a seat;
As a guest-gift, brought him water to wash with,
Enquired of his health;
And at the end of the usual exchanges,
Smiled shyly:
'Now what can I do for you?'

Pleased with the welcome,
Aware of her body—
Its seeming perfection—
The king replied to that short, sweet speech:
'Where's His Holiness, the great seer Kaṇva?
He's the one I've come to worship.
Tell me, if you can, you beautiful creature.'

'My reverend father,' Śakuntalā said,
'Has gone to gather fruit outside the enclosure.
Wait here a while, and you'll see him come back.'

But the king had no interest left in the seer,
He had seen the girl . . .
Her rounded hips, her shining body—
Impossibly beautiful—
Her innocent smile,
Radiant from penance, from self-restraint.

So now he asked her,
So shapely and youthful:
'Who are you? *Whose* are you?
Why, slender child, have you come to this wood,
When you were born with such beauty?
Where do you come from, you radiant creature?
A single glance and my heart's a prisoner:
One thing only I want to know—
Everything about you.'

Questioned like this by a king in a hermitage,
She laughed and spoke sweetly:
'Duṣyanta, I'm the daughter 15
Of the reverend Kaṇva,
Yes—that famous ascetic,
Who knows the Law.'*

'That can't be true . . .
This great and holy man,
Whom the whole world worships,
Has always practised semen retention.*
Law itself might stray from the path,
But not this saint from an avowed intention.
You're beautiful, my dear,
But how can you be his daughter?
No, I can't believe it. And yet . . .
You could try to convince me.'

'Listen, king, and I'll tell you my story
From the very beginning. Then you'll believe
I'm the sage's daughter.

'A seer came here once, like you,
Asking awkward questions about my birth.
I'll repeat, word for word, what Kaṇva told him:

You've heard, I suppose, of Viśvāmitra, 20
The legendary sage, who performed such penance
He seriously mortified Indra himself,

Lord of the gods? Well, Indra, a sacker of cities,
Feared that ascetic, so fired up by his practice—
Feared his power to oust him from heaven.
So he took aside Menakā
And said something like this:

'In you, above all, I can see all the divine qualities
Of a heavenly nymph. Be good to me, lady,
And do as I ask . . .
Viśvāmitra has tapped the power of the sun.
His practice has such charge, it makes my mind spin.
Slender lady, this Viśvāmitra is your target:
He's been piling up terrible austerities—
So terrible, I'm afraid he'll topple my throne.
Go to this sage who has filed his soul
To an invincible core,
And seduce him.
Block his asceticism—do it for me!
Beguile him with your beauty, your youth, your sweetness,
Your gestures, your smiling, your sweet conversation—
Divert his austerities, like the nymph you are!'

Menakā replied:
'As you well know, my lord, that reverend man
Is a great ascetic, packed with energy,
And bad-tempered to boot.
If you're afraid of his power,
His penance, and his temper,
Shouldn't I fear them too?
*This is the man who parted the venerable Vasiṣṭha**
From his beloved sons, who was born a warrior
*And, by sheer force, became a brahmin,**
Who turned the sacred river Kauśiki
Into an impassable torrent
*Just for a wash . . .**
This man has really done these things
And he fills me with dread.

'So perhaps you can tell me, my lord,

How I can escape being burnt by his rage,
When with his kind of power
He could kindle the universe,
Splinter the earth by stamping,
Knead great Mount Meru like a clay-fired top,*
And set it spinning through the sky?.
How could a girl even dare to touch
Such a smouldering, concentrated saint?

'His mouth is the pit for the offering,
His eyes are the moon and the sun,
His tongue is Time—
So how can I hope to move him?
If Yama and Soma, if the greatest seers,*
If all the demigods and guardians of the sun
Stand in such fear, why shouldn't I?

'Yet if you will it,
Then I shall have to approach him . . .
But for a serious attempt
You must take care to protect me.
I'll need a wind to part my skirt,
Just as I'm dancing before him,
And, by your favour, help from the God of Love.
Yes—and a fragrant breeze should blow through the forest
At the crucial time.'

'Of course.'

And so it was arranged,
And so she left for Viśvāmitra's grove.

As Menakā had wanted, 1.66.1
Indra ordered up the restless wind
To help her. Warily, she approached Viśvāmitra,
Performing penance in his ashram—
Practising still, although all his sins
Had long since turned to ash.

She greeted him,
Began to dance;
The wind whipped in,
Removed her moon pale skirt;
Stooping, but against the breeze,
She made to save it, smiling coyly.
And so it was that that supreme ascetic
Saw Menakā naked,
Clutching her skirt,
Seeming so nervous,
Young, and beautiful beyond description.

He couldn't help it,
The power of her beauty
Engulfed him.
Suddenly in love,
He longed to possess her.
She accepted
Without inhibition.
They were lost in the woods,
Making love as it took them,
Months may have passed,
But, for them,
Time had stopped.

And it was there, in a beautiful
Himālayan valley, by the Mālinī river,
That they engendered Śakuntalā,
Their daughter—no sooner born
Than abandoned on the banks of that torrent,
When the nymph, her mission accomplished,
Flew back to heaven.

It was the great birds that saved her:
Seeing a baby, alone in the wilderness,
At the mercy of marauding lions and tigers,
They surrounded Menakā's child to shield her
From carnivores, from beasts of prey.

And it was there that I found her,
When I came to bathe in the river—
A child in a desert place,
Surrounded by birds . . .
I took her home,
*Adopted her, made her my daughter,**
And because the birds of the wilderness
Had saved her,
*Called her 'Śakuntalā'.**

So you can be sure, good brahmin,
Śakuntalā is my daughter,
And considers me her father
In the most innocent way.

'Such is the history of my birth
As Kaṇva described it to the seer.
So you see, my lord, I *am* Kaṇva's daughter,
For I think of Kaṇva as my father,
Never having known my own.

'And now I've told you my story,
Just as I heard it.'

'Beautiful girl, 1.67.1
From what you've said, it's clear
That you're descended from princes . . .*
Marry me,
And then say what I can give you.
Golden necklaces and earrings,
Clothes, and gems from the world's four corners
Are yours for the asking—
Breastplates, hides, anything at all.
Indeed, my kingdom itself
Can be yours, today!
So marry me, lady!
Come to me by the gāndharva rite—*
For, as everyone says,
A gāndharva marriage is best.'

'Lord, my father is out of the hermitage, 5
Gathering fruit. Wait just a while, and he himself
Will give me away.'*

'You must love me—
Don't doubt my commitment—
I've given my heart.

'You are your own kinsman,
You can, of your own volition, have what you want—
You can, quite legally, give yourself away.*
There are eight established
And lawful forms of marriage;
Among them, the gāndharva,
Prescribed for princes.*
And since we love each other,
The solution is obvious:
You should become my wife
By the gāndharva rite.'

'If this is legal, and if I am my own mistress, 15
Then, Puru Lord, before I give myself away,
You must meet this condition:
Promise me faithfully that you'll honour
This contract, made in private between us:
That any son I give birth to
Shall be your immediate heir.
Swear it on oath!
And then, and only then, Duṣyanta,
May you lie with me.'

Without hesitation, the king replied:
'I swear it! Moreover,
You shall come to my city, sweet-smiling girl,
As is your right—you have my word.'
And so he took that graceful lady's hand
And led her to bed.

And later, before his departure, 20

He assured and reassured her
She could trust him—
That he would send an army,
Four divisions strong,
To bring her to his palace—
'Sweet-smiling girl'.

This was how he left her.
But on his journey back, he wondered
How Kaṇva would take the news
Of what had happened in his absence—
He had such powers . . .
And with this on his mind,
Entered his city.

Meanwhile, Kaṇva Kāśyapa himself
Returned to the hermitage,
But Śakuntalā was too embarrassed
To go out and greet him.
Kaṇva, however, a great ascetic;
Had access to knowledge
Through divination;
He knew everything already.
And what he saw pleased him:

'Your making love with this man, 25
Without my permission,
Doesn't violate law.
You are, after all, a prince's daughter,
And a gāndharva marriage
Is the one for your class: "done in secret
Between two lovers, unaccompanied by mantras",
In the words of the book.

'In Duṣyanta, you've chosen a man of stature,
Noble and close to the Law.
He loves you, Śakuntalā—between you,
You'll give the world a brilliant son,

Who shall rule the earth from sea to sea;
An invincible emperor, with universal sway.'

The hermit was weary—
She took his burden,
Sorted the fruit,
Washed the dust from his feet,
Then addressed him:

'Since you agree I've chosen
The right kind of husband,
Please grant his ministers
And my lord himself
Your favour.'

'For your sake
I have been good to them already.
For his sake, now,
Whatever wish you wish,
I shall grant it.'

And because she wanted to help Duṣyanta,
Śakuntalā asked that the descendants of Puru
Should always act virtuously
And never fall from their kingship.

Duṣyanta, his promises promised, 1.68.1
Had been back in his capital
A full three years before Śakuntalā gave birth—
But, to what a son!
Quite boundless in vigour,
Radiant as fire, Duṣyanta's true heir,
With all the royal virtues
Of beauty and bounty.
Kaṇva, best qualified by merit,
Performed the boy's birth rites,
And his other rites too.
He was a boy with leonine power,
Teeth that gleamed like mountain peaks,

Huge strength, a domed and noble head;
And on his palms,
The world-emperor's wheel.*

He grew rapidly, that godlike child,
Raised in the forest. At six,
He had a menagerie of boars,
Buffaloes, lions, tigers, and elephants;
He tied them to the trees of Kaṇva's hermitage,
Broke them in and and rode them ragged—
Just for amusement.
So the hermits called him 'Sarvadamana'—
'All Tamer'; and such was his vigour,
His courage and strength,
The name became his.

Watching this boy
And his prodigious behaviour,
The seer told his mother:
'Now is the time to make him
Heir to the kingdom.'

And seeing how the child strengthened,
Almost minute by minute,
Kaṇva said to his pupils:
'Be swift—take Śakuntalā and her son
From the hermitage to her husband,
Where she may be honoured
For all her best qualities.
Besides, it's not good for women
To live too long with their kinsmen:
Their reputation, conduct, and morals
Are called into question.* Therefore,
Escort her now, without hesitation.'

'At once', they replied, setting out,
With Śakuntalā and Sarvadamana at their head,
For 'The Elephant City', Hastināpura.*

In this way, the beautiful lady
Took her lotus-eyed boy,
So like the child of Immortals,
From the forest where Duṣyanta
Had met her, to the king in the city.

And there, in the city,
She was given recognition,
And with her son,
Dazzling as the light at morning,
Ushered in to see the king.

Śakuntalā paid him the expected honours, then spoke: 15
'This is your son, sir. Consecrate him
As your heir. For it was you, great man,
Who begot this godlike child on me.
Now honour your promise—
That promise you made
As we lay entwined
In Kaṇva's forest retreat,
One afternoon, so many years ago.'

As she spoke, he remembered it
Clearly, but said: 'I recall no such thing.
Whose woman are you, disgraced ascetic?
I remember no business with you at all,
For Law, love, or profit.*
Go, or stay, if that's what you want—
But you can go to hell, for all I care!'

Even a woman of such spirit 20
Was confounded; stunned
With grief, she stood there
Fixed like a pillar.
Then her eyes turned coppery
With ire, her pursed lips
Began to tremble,
She fired glances at the king
That should have burnt him.

But, somehow, though broiling with anger,
She controlled her expression,
And held back the power
She had acquired through penance.
Reflecting a moment,
In sorrow and chagrin,
She faced her husband directly,
And said this through her fury:

'You know what you know, great king!
So why deny it, so cooly,
Lying like a commoner,
Like one of the people?
Your heart knows the difference 25
Between truth and deception.
You, alas, are your only witness—
Don't lie to yourself!
The hypocrite, who knows he's one thing
And pretends he's another,
Is a thief who steals his very own soul—
No crime is beyond him.

'You think, "I am alone",
Forgetting that silent, primaeval seer
Who lives in your heart.
He knows your bad deeds!
He sees your deceit!

'An evil-doer thinks, "None knows it was me."
But he's wrong!
The inner self knows,
The gods know,
The Sun and Moon know,
Wind and Fire, Heaven, Earth and Water,
Day, Night, Dawn and Dusk, the Law,
Death and the Heart
All know his business,
And that of every man.
The God of Death dissolves a man's bad deeds 30

If his all-seeing conscience is clear.
But if that inner witness is anguished,
Torn by its soul's wickedness,
Death bears the miscreant away.

'So the soul is no help, and the gods of no benefit,
To the hypocrite who denies himself
And dissembles to others.

'I've been a faithful wife—
Just because I'm here alone,
Don't try to discount me.
You've neglected what was due to any guest,
Let alone your own spouse,
Here of her own free will!
Why do you ignore me before your assembly,
Am I a commoner?
Is this a void?
Am I talking to myself?
Why don't you listen?
Pay attention, Duṣyanta, or—
I'm warning you—
Your head will burst into a hundred pieces,*
Before I've finished this speech!

'A husband enters his wife,
And, as a result, is born again.
According to the ancient poets,
That is what wives are for.
By bearing children to the man who enters her,*
She extends his lineage
And saves his ancestors who died before.*
(Svayaṃbhū, himself, has said a son is called *putra*
Because he saves his father from the hell called Put.)*

'What is a wife?
A woman who is useful in the house,
Who bears children,
Whose husband is her very life,

Loyal—a man's other half,
And his closest companion,
The root of his life's unfolding,
His solace when dying.
Those who marry can do their ritual duty,*
Set up a household, be fortunate and happy.
A sweet-spoken wife is a friend to the solitary,
A father in ritual, a mother in suffering;
In the wilderness, she brings ease
To the man who is journeying.
A man with a wife is a man to be trusted;
Therefore a wife is the prize above prizes.

'The faithful wife alone follows her husband
Through dangers—through death itself,
And beyond, into transmigration;
She is always his wife:
If she dies before him,
She halts and awaits him:
If he goes first, then she follows after.
This, sir, is why men want to get married:
To gain a wife here
And hereafter.

'According to those who ought to know, a son
Is the man himself reborn.
So a man thinks of his son's mother
As his own. His wife's son
Is his own face in a mirror.
Gazing on him, he's euphoric—
A saint reaching heaven.
Suffering men, consumed by heart's sorrow,
Rejoice in their wives, as the parched
Drink water. However provoked, the wise man
Says nothing to offend a woman,
In her he sees his love, his joy, his merit.
Women are the eternal, sacred field of being—
Who, even among seers,
Can produce children without them?

What greater joy for a man than a little son,
Who plays in the dust,
Then covers him in grubby kisses?*

'So why do you scorn that child,
Who has come to you freely
And looks at you with love?
Ants carry their eggs and never break them—
Yet you, who are versed in the Law,
Can't bear your own son?
The feel of a dress, of a lover,
Of water, are none of them sweeter
Than the touch of a son.
Among humans, brahmins are best;
Among beasts, the cow;
Of those due respect, the guru is greatest;
And of what can be touched, a son.

'Hug this handsome son of yours!
There is nothing better in the earth or on it
Than the touch of your very own son.
For three long years I bore this boy
To destroy your sorrow.
Then, at his birth, a voice from the sky called to me:
"A hundred times he'll sacrifice the horse."*

'Why, men who've been no further than the next village
Return and take their sons onto their laps with love,
Nuzzle their heads, and thrill with joy.
Brahmins, as you know,
Recite these Vedic verses
At birth rites for their boys:

Limb by limb you come into being,
Out of my essence you are born,
You are myself, though called my son—
Live for a hundred years!

My nurture depends on you alone,
Through you alone my line endures.

So be happy, be happy my son,
And live for a hundred years!

'He was born from your body:
A man from a man.
Look on my son as your second self,
A reflection in a pellucid pond.
Just as the fire for the offerings
Is kindled from the household fire,
So he is born from you,
And what was single is doubled.

'Once, king, when I was young,
And you were out hunting,
You followed a deer to my father's retreat,
Where I was then living . . .
Urvaśī, Pūrvacitti, Sahajanyā, and Menakā,
Viśvācī and Ghṛtācī are the six supreme
Celestial nymphs. Of those,
It was the beautiful Menakā,
Brahmā's daughter, who came from heaven
To earth, and bore me by Viśvāmitra.
That nymph gave birth to me in the high Himālayas,
Then discarded me and disappeared—
I might have been a stranger's child.

'What evil deeds I must have done
In other lives, to be abandoned by my kin
In infancy, and now again by you!
If you're determined to disown me,
I'll return to the hermitage,
But this child, you should not forsake—
For he is your very own son.'

Duṣyanta replied:
'I do not know, Śakuntalā, that you've given birth
To any son of mine. Women are liars—
Who can believe a word you say?
We're expected to think that Menakā,

Your mother, was a compassionless whore
Who cast you off like a bleached garland
On a Himālayan peak?
That Viśvāmitra, your unfeeling father,
The prince who made himself into a brahmin,
Was a libertine, whose real business was lust?

'Menakā is the greatest of the celestial nymphs, 75
Your "father" the greatest of seers—
And you say you're their child,
When you speak like a slut?

'Aren't you ashamed to utter
Such brazen drivel, and before my face?
Disappear, bogus ascetic!
What have a dreadful seer and a nymph
Like Menakā to do with you—
A wretch disguised as a nun?

'As for your boy, he's far too big—
So strong, and yet still a child?
Did he shoot up like a rampant weed,
Overnight?

'You must have been born in the gutter—
You certainly look like a slut to me!
And you claim to have been Menakā's love child?
Nothing you say makes sense, "ascetic". 80
You mean nothing to me. Just go—
Who cares where, apart from you?'

Śakuntalā replied: 1.69.1
'You can see a fault like a mustard seed
In someone else, but in yourself,
Sins large as pumpkins go through on the nod.
Menakā is pre-eminent among the thirty gods—*
That makes me better born than you!
You are tied to the earth, Duṣyanta,
I wander the skies: I am Mount Meru
To your grain of sand. The palaces of the mighty—

Indra, Kubera, Yama, and Varuṇa—*
Are my second home and stamping-ground,
Such is my power!
What I have to tell you is simple and true:
I do it to instruct you, faultless king,
Not to spite. Be patient.
Listen:

'As long as he doesn't face himself
In the mirror, a repulsive man thinks,
"I'm better than the common crowd",
But in a glass, he sees at once
It's really ugliness that marks him out.
Most handsome in a man
Is never to think badly of others;
The gossip, on the other hand, is just a step
From foul-mouthed slander.
A fool, hearing the world's chatter—
Good and evil mixed,
Snaffles up the evil,
Like a pig truffling ordure.
The wise man discriminates:
Hearing chatterers rake through good and bad,
He picks out the good—a goose
Siphoning milk from water.*
As much as it pains the virtuous
To criticize others, so the bad
Enjoy it. Just as the good
Take delight in speaking well of their elders,
So fools amuse themselves, traducing the decent.
Fools try to find out
Others' faults—better by far
To be unaware.
When men speak ill of the good,
It's the fool who tags along behind, saying:
"He's *my* enemy too!"
What could be more ludicrous
Than sinners slandering the good?
Forget the devout, even atheists

Recoil from the man who cares nothing for truth,
As though they'd seen a poisonous snake,
About to strike.

'The man who refuses recognition
To the son he's fathered as his equal,
Shall see the gods destroy his fortune,
And never reach the heavenly kingdoms.
For the ancestors call a son
The family line's support,
The apogee of universal order—
Never, never abandon a son!
Fathers of sons earn the respect
Due to a man who's done his social duty—
Sons swell the love in their father's hearts,
And ferry their ancestors out of hell*
On the raft of filial devotion.

'Tigerish king, if you would preserve
The truth, the Law, and yourself,
Don't abandon your son!
Lionlike lord, don't stoop to deceit!
A pond is better than a hundred wells,
A sacrifice better than a hundred ponds,
A son better than a hundred rites,
But truth—truth counts for more than even a hundred sons.

'If a thousand horse sacrifices and a true word
Were put in the balance: the word would be heavier.
Learning the entire Veda,*
And bathing at every sacred ford,
May or may not be its equal,
But nothing exceeds the truth—
No higher law is known to man.
And there is nothing more corrosive on earth
Than a lie.
Truth, king, is the Supreme Reality,
The highest rule of life.

Don't abandon that rule, my lord:
Don't abandon your ally!

'But if you must cling to your lie,
If you can't, of your own accord,
Believe me,
Then I shall leave you.
For there's no keeping company
With your kind of man.
But with or without you, Duṣyanta,
My son shall rule this four-cornered earth,
With the king of the mountains,
The Himālaya itself, as his crown!'

So Śakuntalā ended, and left.

Then, out of the sky, a voice addressed Duṣyanta
As he sat in his court:
'The mother carries the father's life-giving water—*
It is the father who begets the son.
Treasure your son, Duṣyanta—
A fertile son saves from the house of Death.
Don't repudiate Śakuntalā,
She spoke the truth:
You seeded her womb.

'A wife splits her body to give birth to a child
Therefore, Duṣyanta, treasure Śakuntalā's son,
Or welcome disaster!
What man alive would abandon
A living boy, born from himself?
Paurava, treasure Duṣyanta and Śakuntalā's
Great son. He shall be called "Bharata", "Sustained",*
Since you must sustain him!'

Delight was the Paurava king's reaction
To this decree from the gods.
Turning to his chaplain and ministers he said:

'Mark, sirs, what this emissary of the gods
Has spoken. I, too, knew very well
This was my son. But had I recognized him
On nothing but his mother's word,
He would never have been free
Of the people's suspicion.'

So the king, prompted by the gods,
Made doubt redundant and received his son
With happiness and joy—kissed his head,
Hugged him with love—
While brahmins gave him a brahmin welcome
And bards sang songs of praise.
At the touch of his son, the king
Was enraptured,
But, knowing his duty to his wife,
He honoured her as she deserved,
And made this soothing speech:

'Our union was hidden from the people;
That's why I debated, my queen,
To clear you of blame. Otherwise,
They might have said some woman I'd seduced
Was using me to ease her son onto the throne.
That's why I argued.
And if you have spoken to me harshly,
In anger, I know how much it came from love,
And I forgive you, freely, my sweet wife.'

Saying this to his beloved queen,
King Duṣyanta honoured her with clothing,
Food, and drink. Then he named
His son by beautiful Śakuntalā, 'Bharata',
And anointed him his designated heir.

So the glorious chariot wheel
Of great-souled Bharata
Rolled about the echoing world—
Huge, radiant, divine, unconquered.

He defeated the lords of the earth,
And made them his vassals;
He lived a just life, and attained high fame.
He was king and emperor,
Glorious monarch of the spreading earth,
Lavish in his sacrifices, an Indra,
A lord of the whirling winds.
Like Dakṣa, he had Kaṇva perform a sacrifice*
Priced at a thousand, thousand cows.

From Bharata flowed the fame of the Bhāratas,
From Bharata the Bhārata line,
And all the ancients famed as Bhāratas,
Godlike and powerful,
Truth-telling kings.*

EXPLANATORY NOTES

THE RECOGNITION OF ŚAKUNTALĀ BY KĀLIDĀSA

The primary purpose of these notes is to explain Indological references to the non-expert reader, although a general understanding of the play is by no means dependent upon them. They are not intended to provide a thematic commentary; for some general remarks of that kind, see the Introduction.

Prologue

Goethe, a great enthusiast for *Śakuntalā*, was so impressed by this device that he borrowed it for the opening of his *Faust, Part One.*

5 *Benediction*: because it is a blessing, the benediction could only normally be spoken by a brahmin. If the Actor-Manager of the troupe was qualified in this respect, then he would have done it, *as a brahmin*; only after he had spoken it would he have gone into character as the 'Actor-Manager' in the play. (Numeration of verses follows Kale's edition of the Devanāgarī recension; verses followed by a letter (e.g. 14a) indicate material he prints in his notes (often identical with the Bengali recension) but excludes from his main text.)

eight . . . Śiva: i.e. eight visible forms of the great Hindu god Śiva. In the original playhouse this benediction would have marked the end of a series of lengthy ritual preliminaries to the performance. See David Gitomer, 'The Theater in Kālidāsa's Art', in B.S. Miller (ed.), *The Theater of Memory: The Plays of Kālidāsa* (New York: Columbia University Press, 1984), 65 ff.

the curtain: i.e. looking towards the green room. See section on 'Staging and Stage Conventions' in the Introduction.

6 *Ravished . . . away*: this is what aesthetic rapture is supposed to do to the audience, and will do to the king—obliterate everything else, including memory.

Duṣyanta: for the sake of consistency, I have used this form of the king's name throughout both the play and the *Mahābhārata* episode. Some manuscripts, and the critical edition of the *Mahābhārata* (which I have altered in this translation), use the Sanskrit form 'Duḥṣanta'.

Act 1

7 *Śiva . . . the chase*: in a well-known myth, Śiva, taking revenge for his exclusion from the gods' sacrifice (also known as 'Dakṣa's sacrifice'), disrupts the ritual and hunts down the sacrifice, which has fled away in the form of a deer. See Stella Kramrisch, *The Presence of Śiva* (Princeton: Princeton University Press, 1981), 322–40.

Darbha grass: = kusha, a type of grass frequently used in sacrificial rituals.

8 *Indra's steeds*: Indra is the king of the gods in the early Vedic hymns and in post-Vedic mythology. In terms of religious significance, however, Śiva, Viṣṇu, and the Goddess are the great deities of classical Hinduism. The king will actually be riding a chariot drawn by Indra's horses in Act 7.

9 *Puru's race*: Puru is the progenitor of the Lunar Dynasty to which Duṣyanta belongs (see next note).

Lunar Dynasty: with the Solar, one of the two great dynasties of ancient India according to Hindu mythology.

a son . . . to rule the world: a 'world-emperor' or *cakravartin* ('wheel-turning monarch'), a ruler whose divine powers and influence are reflected in his physical appearance. See the king's description of his son (p. 95), whose birth fulfills this prophetic wish. Cf. 'Śakuntalā in the *Mahābhārata*', pp. 124 f.

Somatīrtha . . . fate: Somatīrtha is a pilgrimage site on the coast of Gujarat, associated with the moon (Soma), and distant enough to keep Kaṇva out of the way until Act 4. Cf. 'Śakuntalā in the *Mahābhārata*', p. 116, where Kaṇva is simply gathering fruit outside the hermitage, necessitating a lightning seduction. We are never told the precise nature of Śakuntalā's 'hostile fate', but it seems to be a precognition of Durvāsas's curse in Act 4. If so, Kaṇva's pilgrimage seems to have been, at best, only partially successful.

10 *iṅgudi nuts*: pounded by forest-dwelling ascetics to produce oil for lamps and medicinal ointments.

bark garments: traditional ascetic dress, as complained of by Śakuntalā (pp. 11 f.).

ghee: clarified butter used in rituals.

this vein . . . woman's charm: a throbbing right arm is an omen of an erotic encounter for a man, perhaps leading to marriage.

12 *'sweet talker'*: the literal meaning of Priyaṃvadā's name.

jasmine . . . as her bridegroom: so the bride has chosen the bridegroom, a form of marriage permissible for princesses (Śakuntalā is a royal sage's daughter). Cf. p. 51.

13 *woman of a different class*: if Śakuntalā's parents are both of the brahmin class, then she too must marry a brahmin. That would make her ineligible for the king, who belongs to the princely or warrior class. However, since her real father was Viśvāmitra, a *royal* sage, she too is really of the princely class, and the king's fears are ungrounded, as he discovers below.

14 *Paurava king*: i.e. Duṣyanta himself.

15 *our hermitage*: this speech seems an increasingly formal and desperate attempt to engage the king in conversation, when he is probably in rapt contemplation of Śakuntalā and largely oblivious to everything else.

15 *erotic attraction*: see the Introduction, section on 'Staging and Stage Conventions'.

16 *Kauśika*: i.e. Viśvāmitra. Cf. the concise and allusive account of Śakuntalā's birth and parenthood, given here, with the much fuller version, given by Śakuntalā herself, in the *Mahābhārata* (pp. 117 f.).

deep meditation: such practices were thought to generate supernatural powers that could rival or surpass those possessed by the gods. Cf. 'Śakuntalā in the *Mahābhārata*, pp. 117–18.

17 *foothold at last*: he knows now that they are of the same class.

18 *the venerable Gautamī*: the senior female ascetic.

Act 2

21 *the Vidūṣaka*: a stock character in Sanskrit drama, sometimes referred to in translation as 'the Buffoon'. Although he has some things in common with Shakespeare's clowns, he is in fact a brahmin, although a caricature of one: overweight, bald, and hunchbacked. As in this act, he usually carries a crooked stick.

attendant girls: the term in Sanskrit is *yavanī*, usually taken to refer to Greek (Ionian) women from Asia Minor who had settled in Bactria, and who acted as the king's bow- and arrow-bearers. Some scholars think the term had a wider use and was never restricted to Greeks.

22 *reed . . . hunchback*: a reference by the Vidūṣaka to himself (he is hunchbacked).

23 *with relish*: traditionally the Vidūṣaka has an excessively sweet tooth.

considered a vice: according to the Hindu law books, hunting is one of the four most pernicious vices of the ten that afflict kings, on a par with drinking, womanizing, and gambling: see Wendy Doniger, with Brian K. Smith (trans.), *The Laws of Manu* (Harmondsworth: Penguin Books, 1991), 7. 47–50.

25 *sunstones*: crystals that were believed to ignite when caught by the sun.

26 *arka's pliant leaf*: the arka is a plant with large leaves, associated with the sacrificial ritual, hence its correspondence in the simile to a priestly sage.

30 *Triśaṅku*: a mythical king who wanted to ascend to heaven in his physical body. The royal sage Viśvāmitra (Śakuntalā's real father) was persuaded to perform the necessary rituals. Indra and the gods, however, would not accept Triśaṅku in heaven and hurled him back, whereupon Viśvāmitra suspended him, head down, halfway between earth and sky, where he remains as a constellation (the 'Southern Cross').

Act 3

32 *reduced you to ash*: Kāma, the God of Love, tried to disturb Śiva when he was engaged in meditation, whereupon the great yogi incinerated him with heat from his third eye, making Kāma bodiless.

34 *slips her wrist*: as in the West, love-sickness is seen as a kind of illness, but in the Indian context it is expressed specifically in terms of bodily emaciation (male and female), which, if unremedied, may result in death. In the play such emaciation, while strengthening the erotic mood, also echoes the result of the austerities performed by the hermitage ascetics.

36 *double stars of spring*: a constellation. Apparently a reference to the two friends' service to Śakuntalā, but also, perhaps, through their championing of his suit, their service to the king, since he belongs to the Lunar Dynasty.

37 *goddess Lakṣmī*: the goddess of wealth and good fortune, and so riches personified.

39 *Kāma's dart*: Kāma is the God of Love.

earth: the king, as king, is thought to be married to the earth, who is a goddess.

40 *the law . . . done*: the king is suggesting a *gāndharva* form of marriage, glossed by Kaṇva in the 'Śakuntalā in the *Mahābhārata*' episode as 'done in secret between two lovers, unaccompanied by mantras' (p. 123). Effectively, it means sexual intercourse by mutual consent, an arrangement which, although unconventional, has legal force as a form of marriage for couples from the princely class.

Red goose . . . gander: pairs of sheldrakes—red geese—are said to be inseparable by day, but cursed to be parted at night.

Act 4

44 *slight a guest, do you?*: hospitality is a fundamental socio-religious duty for Hindus, and its neglect a serious fault.

47 *fire . . . wood*: this refers to a myth in which Fire (Agni) enters into a tree to prevent himself being burnt up by Śiva's fiery seed, which he is carrying on behalf of the gods. Fire was thereafter thought to be ever-present in wood, from which it may be kindled for sacrificial and other purposes. The verse is in Sanskrit, which is how Priyaṃvadā, normally a Prakrit speaker, relays it to her friend.

Hastināpura: Duṣyanta's capital, said to have been north-east of modern Delhi.

'Great Queen': the queen whose eldest son becomes heir to the throne.

48 *mental power*: his superhuman yogic power.

49 *back from bathing now*: not a recreational or hygienic bath, but part of a brahmin's daily rituals.

Śakuntalā . . . must leave today: according to traditional Indian critics, this verse, embedded in the play's core act, represents its aesthetic essence—the epitome and perfection of *kāvya*.

50 *Śarmiṣṭhā to Yayāti*: Śarmiṣṭhā was Yayāti's queen by a *gāndharva* marriage, and her husband's favourite, although initially a junior wife; their

youngest son was Duṣyanta's ancestor, Puru, a universal emperor. See the *Mahābhārata*, 1. 70–80.

50 *Vedic metre*: this is essentially a marriage rite without the bridegroom, accompanied by an appropriately Vedic-sounding mantra.

52 *kusha*: = *darbha* grass (see note to p. 7).

53 *Without her mate*: see note to p. 40.

Act 5

57 *Queen Vasumatī*: Vasumatī and Haṃsapadikā are two of Duṣyanta's queens, between whom he is obviously transferring his affections now his memory of Śakuntalā has been wiped by the sage's curse. Haṃsapadikā's song, however, is clearly meant to evoke the king's treatment of Śakuntalā in the minds of the audience.

my tuft of hair: the tuft of hair or topknot worn by brahmins is one sign of their orthodox status, and is only shaved if they take full renunciation. It marks the place where the soul is supposed to leave the body at death.

60 *I feel . . . beggar's gaze*: i.e. someone in a state of purity suddenly subject to pollution from contact with a low-caste or polluted individual.

61 *my right eyelid tremble so?*: in contrast to the king's trembling arm in Act 1 (p. 10), throbbing on the right side of the body is considred an evil omen for a woman.

62 *and then says this . . .*: the end of a stream of formal greetings.

63 *with her husband*: Śārṅgarava's words here seem to echo those of Kaṇva in the *Mahābhārata* episode, 'Besides, it's not good for women . . .' (p. 125).

68 *bodily signs of a Universal Emperor*: see note to p. 9.

Act 6

70 *a pure profession!*: said sarcastically, of course. Because it involves the pollutions of violence and death, fishing is an occupation associated with the lowest, and therefore most impure castes.

71 *dog of death*: a reference to the God of Death's canine companions.

72 *You're really . . . of wine*: in the Bengali recension the equivalent speech (in a different Prakrit) is given to Jānuka (the Second Policeman), and it seems much more likely to be his than that the Chief would suddenly become familiar with a low-caste fisherman. Directors might wish to reallocate the speech on these lines.

spring festival: held in honour of Kāma, the God of Love.

73 *of his five*: floral arrows.

deserted young wives: i.e. women thought to be particularly vulnerable to the pangs of love.

tossing the curtain aside: so entering suddenly and angrily.

77 *hide behind the creepers*: since she has already made herself invisible, it is

not clear why she needs to do this, unless to give a dramatic echo to the king's concealment in Act 1.

78 *good actions at once?*: i.e. the karmic recompense for his previous good deeds manifesting, and so exhausting itself suddenly. This is based on the idea that all significant actions, in this and previous lives, have future but finite consequences, good and bad, depending on the moral quality of such actions ('the law of karma').

84 *his first love's feelings*: those of Queen Vasumatī.

85 *the ritual to ensure the birth of a son*: a reference to the *puṃsavaṇa* rite—a life-cycle ritual performed in the third month of pregnancy. On the importance of sons in classical Indian and Hindu culture, see the Introduction, section on 'Aesthetic Theory and the Meaning of *Śakuntalā*'. The legal assumption underlying this passage is that when a man dies without a male heir, it is the king rather than the man's family that inherits.

86 *the offering*: part of the offering made by their eldest male descendant (the king, in this case) at the ceremony for the dead, known as the *śrāddha* rite, the purpose of which is to feed the ancestors in the afterlife.

Brahminicide!: to kill a Brahmin, 'a god on earth', is far worse than other kinds of homicide (according to Brahminical Law).

88 *a goose . . . of water*: the wild goose has the proverbial ability to separate milk from any water it may be mixed with.

Kālanemi: a demon opposed to the gods.

Nārada: a great seer who appears in numerous epic stories.

Act 7

90 *Jayanta*: Indra's son.

Viṣṇu . . . claws: in his incarnation (*avatāra*) in the form of the man-lion, the great god Viṣṇu destroyed the demon king Hiraṇyakaśipu, who was claiming Indra's throne.

91 *the wind, Parivaha*: according to Hindu cosmology, the atmosphere is divided into seven paths, each with its own wind; Parivaha is the sixth wind, created by the second of the great god Viṣṇu's cosmic strides in his dwarf (Vāmana) incarnation: i.e. his stride through the atmosphere (the others encompassed earth and heaven). For a brief account of this myth, see the entry under 'Vāmana' in Margaret and James Stutley, *A Dictionary of Hinduism* (London: Routledge & Kegan Paul, 1977). Parivaha is the wind that bears the three streams of the heavenly Ganges (the Milky Way), and the seven stars of the Great Bear.

92 *Mārīca . . . demons*: Mārīca (also known as Kaśyapa and Prajāpati) is the grandson of the divine demiurge Brahmā, and plays an essential part in creation. (His parentage of gods and demons is mentioned here.) He and Aditi are the parents of Indra, the king of the gods. Kaṇva is a descendant of Mārīca and, in the play, his terrestrial analogue.

93 *the responsibilities of a devoted wife*: cf. the direct 'sermon' on this delivered by Śakuntalā herself in the *Mahābhārata* episode (pp. 128 ff.).

94 *Throbs in my arm*: a repetition and reminder of the omen the king feels on entering the terrestrial hermitage in Act 1. See note to p. 10.

this cub: cf. 'Śakuntalā in the *Mahābhārata*', p. 125.

95 *palms are webbed*: one of the physical signs of a world-ruler (*cakravartin*); see note on p. 9; cf. 'Śakuntalā in the *Mahābhārata*', pp. 124 f. for further physical indicators; see also A. L. Basham, *The Wonder That Was India* (New York: Grove Press, 1959), 83 ff., on the concept of the world-ruler or universal monarch.

96 *Lucky . . . speech*: this verse seems to be drawn directly from Śakuntalā's speech about sons in the *Mahābhārata* episode, 'What greater joy for a man than a little son . . .' (p. 130).

97 *Where is she?*: because of an ambiguity in the Prakrit used, the boy thinks he has heard them call his mother's name, śakunta being the name of a bird. Cf. 'Śakuntalā in the *Mahābhārata*', p. 121. For a more detailed linguistic explanation see Miller (ed.), *Theater of Memory*, 342.

98 *a single braid*: a sign of her separation from her husband.

99 *Rohiṇī*: the favourite wife of the Moon.

100 *previous life . . . time*: see note to p. 78.

101 *Marīci and Dakṣa*: the parents of Mārīca and Aditi. See note to p. 92.

Twelve forms: the Ādityas, or forms of the sun in each of the twelve months; children of Mārīca and Aditi.

102 *Paulomī*: Indra's wife.

104 *Bharata, Sustainer*: the legendary ruler of the world (traditionally viewed as comprised of seven islands) who gives his name to India (Bharatavarṣa or Bhārata). See 'Śakuntalā in the *Mahābhārata*', pp. 136 f.

105 *Free me . . . Forever*: a wish that the great god Śiva should liberate him from the cycle of rebirths (*saṃsāra*) to which, conditioned by his actions (*karma*), he will otherwise remain bound—an epilogue to mirror the play's opening benediction.

ŚAKUNTALĀ IN THE MAHĀBHĀRATA

109 *a Paurava forefather:* i.e. he belongs to the Puru or Lunar Dynasty (see notes on the play, p. 9). The translation starts at *Mahābhārata*, 1. 62. 3: in the wider context of the epic the sage Vaiśaṃpāyana is telling King Janamejaya about the origins of the Puru or Lunar Dynasty, to which the latter belongs.

To the Āryan limit: i.e. to the edge of the civilized world, defined by the acceptance of the fourfold class structure of the Āryans. 'Āryan' ('Noble') was the self-designation of the people whose language and culture dominated northern India from the middle of the second millennium BCE.

Mount Mandara: a mythical white mountain, used by the gods and anti-gods to churn the ocean, according to a famous myth.

110 *Indra*: see note on *The Recognition of Śakuntalā*, p. 8.

111 *Garuḍa in flight*: Garuḍa is a bird-deity, and Viṣṇu-Kṛṣṇa's vehicle or mount. He is usually depicted with wings or talons and a beaked human face.

114 *Vedic chant:* mantras drawn from the early Vedic texts (considered to be revelation), and an essential part of ritual; evidence, in this case, of the presence of forest-dwelling ascetics.

Nara and Nārāyaṇa's: two legendary seers, whose hermitage was supposed to have been on the upper Ganges (Gaṅgā).

Citraratha's field: Citraratha is the king of the celestial nymphs and musicians; his field is the grove he constructed for the king of the gods Indra.

Indra's heaven: the very place where the king is honoured in Kālidāsa's play: see *The Recognition of Śakuntalā*, p. 90.

115 *world of Brahmā*: the highest of the worlds in traditional cosmology.

Pacing their sacrificial enclosures . . .: vv. 32–7 (on types of ritual specialists and their duties) omitted.

116 *Śrī herself*: good fortune, personified as a goddess.

117 *the Law*: the Sanskrit is *dharma*, a multivalent term signifying the divine order underlying the universe, and its manifestation in human and social structures. See Introduction, section on 'Aesthetic Theory and the Meaning of *Śakuntalā*'.

semen retention: a standard ascetic practice for generating supernormal powers, which would be dissipated by ejaculation.

118 *Vasiṣṭha*: an ancient seer and bitter rival of Viśvāmitra. Viśvāmitra caused Vasiṣṭha's sons to be destroyed by a demonic spirit—see *Mahābhārata*, I. 165.

became a brahmin: to increase his power, since he believed his warrior's power to be too weak; see *Mahābhārata*, I. 165, and note on *The Recognition of Śakuntalā*, p. 13.

Just for a wash: vv. 31–4 (giving more details of Viśvāmitra's previous deeds) omitted.

119 *Mount Meru*: the mountain at the centre of the cosmos; the earth's axis.

Yama and Soma: the God of Death, and the divine personification of the plant whose juice was central to Vedic sacrifice.

121 *made her my daughter*: v. 13 omitted:

> The law, as you know, defines three kinds of father:
> The child's maker,
> The one who rescues her,
> And the one who succours her.

121 *Called her 'Śakuntalā'*: *śakunta*='bird'; cf. *The Recognition of Śakuntalā*, p. 97.

descended from princes . . .: and so eligible to marry him, her real father, Viśvāmitra, having been a member of the warrior class. See note on *The Recognition of Śakuntalā*, p. 13.

the gāndharva rite: see note on *The Recognition of Śakuntalā*, p. 40.

122 *Will give me away*: in Jamison's words, '[Śakuntalā] immediately counters with an appeal to conventional, parentally controlled marriage': Stephanie W. Jamison, *Sacrificed Wife/Sacrificer's Wife: Women, Ritual, and Hospitality in Ancient India* (New York: Oxford University Press, 1996), 249.

give yourself away: the king claims that 'she can act simultaneously as the bride and the giver of the bride, i.e. her father': Jamison, *Sacrificed Wife/Sacrificer's Wife*, 249.

Prescribed for princes: these two lines summarize vv. 8b–14 (on the eight types of marriage), which are omitted. On the gāndharva rite, see note on *The Recognition of Śakuntalā*, p. 40; on the eight forms of marriage, see Jamison, *Sacrificed Wife/Sacrificer's Wife*, 210–12.

125 *world-emperor's wheel*: concludes a list of physical indicators of a *cakravartin* or universal emperor; cf. notes on *The Recognition of Śakuntalā*, pp. 9, 95.

called into question: cf. Śārṅgarava's verse in *The Recognition of Śakuntalā*, p. 63.

Hastināpura: see *The Recognition of Śakuntalā*, note to p. 47.

126 *Law, love, or profit*: the three legitimate worldly pursuits; see Introduction, section on 'Aesthetic Theory and the Meaning of *Śakuntalā*'.

128 *burst into a hundred pieces*: for an analysis of this threat as a means to tracing the origins of the *Mahābhārata* 's version of the Śakuntalā story, see Stanley Insler, 'The Shattered Head Split and the Epic Tale of Śakuntalā', *Bulletin d'Études Indiennes*, 7–8 (1989–90), 97–139.

who enters her: van Buitenen translates this (*āgamavataḥ*) as 'who follows the scriptures'.

ancestors who died before: see note on *The Recognition of Śakuntalā*, p. 86.

Svayaṃbhū . . . Put: a pseudo-etymology of the Sanskrit word for son. Svayaṃbhū is a name for the first Creator.

129 *ritual duty*: a man could not set up the fire necessary for orthodox domestic rituals, or indeed perform them at all, without being married.

130 *grubby kisses?*: cf. Duṣyanta's verse in *The Recognition of Śakuntalā*, pp. 95f.

sacrifice the horse: the horse sacrifice was the most elaborate of the Vedic rituals, and only performed by the most powerful kings. That he would be thought capable of performing a hundred such sacrifices indicates the boy's extraordinary power.

132 *thirty gods*: a rounding down of the Vedic thirty-three; relatively minor deities, such as the Ādityas; see note on *The Recognition of Śakuntalā*, p. 101.

133 *Indra, Kubera, Yama, and Varuṇa*: the lord of the gods, the God of Wealth, the God of Death, and the god associated with celestial order and duty.

milk from water: see note on *The Recognition of Śakuntalā*, p. 88.

134 *out of hell*: by keeping them fed in the afterlife through the offerings of the *śrāddha* ritual; see note on *The Recognition of Śakuntalā*, p. 86.

the entire Veda: the sacred texts of brahminical Hinduism, orally transmitted between brahmins, and regarded as revelation.

135 *life-giving water*: this seems to refer to the sac that receives the father's seed.

"Bharata", "Sustained": usually known, actively, as the 'Sustainer'; see note on *The Recognition of Śakuntalā*, p. 104.

137 *Dakṣa . . . a sacrifice*: Dakṣa is one of the Ādityas (see note on *The Recognition of Śakuntalā*, p. 101) and a legendary sacrificer. The cows are the fee, paid to Kaṇva and other officiating brahmins for their technical services.

Truth-telling kings: a compression of vv. 50–1, eulogizing the Bharata line, and leading into the next episode in the *Mahābhārata*.

A SELECTION OF **OXFORD WORLD'S CLASSICS**

	The Bhagavad Gita
	The Bible Authorized King James Version *With Apocrypha*
	The Koran
	The Pañcatantra
	Upaniṣads
AUGUSTINE	**The Confessions**
	On Christian Teaching
BEDE	**The Ecclesiastical History**
HEMACANDRA	**The Lives of the Jain Elders**
ŚĀNTIDEVA	**The Bodhicaryāvatāra**

A SELECTION OF OXFORD WORLD'S CLASSICS

	The Anglo-Saxon World
	Lancelot of the Lake
	The Paston Letters
	The Romance of Reynard the Fox
	The Romance of Tristan
GEOFFREY CHAUCER	**The Canterbury Tales** **Troilus and Criseyde**
JOCELIN OF BRAKELOND	**Chronicle of the Abbey of Bury St Edmunds**
GUILLAUME DE LORRIS and JEAN DE MEUN	**The Romance of the Rose**
WILLIAM LANGLAND	**Piers Plowman**

A SELECTION OF OXFORD WORLD'S CLASSICS

Thomas Aquinas	**Selected Philosophical Writings**
George Berkeley	**Principles of Human Knowledge and Three Dialogues**
Edmund Burke	**A Philosophical Enquiry into the Origin of Our Ideas of the Sublime and Beautiful** **Reflections on the Revolution in France**
Thomas Carlyle	**The French Revolution**
Confucius	**The Analects**
Friedrich Engels	**The Condition of the Working Class in England**
James George Frazer	**The Golden Bough**
Thomas Hobbes	**Human Nature and De Corpore Politico** **Leviathan**
John Hume	**Dialogues Concerning Natural Religion and The Natural History of Religion** **Selected Essays**
Thomas Malthus	**An Essay on the Principle of Population**
Karl Marx	**Capital** **The Communist Manifesto**
J. S. Mill	**On Liberty and Other Essays** **Principles of Economy and Chapters on Socialism**
Friedrich Nietzsche	**On the Genealogy of Morals** **Twilight of the Idols**
Thomas Paine	**Rights of Man, Common Sense, and Other Political Writings**
Jean-Jacques Rousseau	**Discourse on Political Economy and The Social Contract** **Discourse on the Origin of Inequality**
Sima Qian	**Historical Records**
Adam Smith	**An Inquiry into the Nature and Causes of the Wealth of Nations**
Mary Wollstonecraft	**Political Writings**

A SELECTION OF **OXFORD WORLD'S CLASSICS**

	An Anthology of Elizabethan Prose Fiction
	An Anthology of Seventeenth-Century Fiction
Aphra Behn	**Oroonoko and Other Writings**
John Bunyan	**Grace Abounding** **The Pilgrim's Progress**
Sir Philip Sidney	**The Old Arcadia**
Izaak Walton	**The Compleat Angler**

A SELECTION OF **OXFORD WORLD'S CLASSICS**

Jane Austen	Emma Persuasion Pride and Prejudice Sense and Sensibility
Anne Brontë	The Tenant of Wildfell Hall
Charlotte Brontë	Jane Eyre
Emily Brontë	Wuthering Heights
Wilkie Collins	The Woman in White
Joseph Conrad	Heart of Darkness Nostromo
Charles Darwin	The Origin of Species
Charles Dickens	Bleak House David Copperfield Great Expectations Hard Times
George Eliot	Middlemarch The Mill on the Floss
Elizabeth Gaskell	Cranford
Thomas Hardy	Jude the Obscure
Walter Scott	Ivanhoe
Mary Shelley	Frankenstein
Robert Louis Stevenson	Treasure Island
Bram Stoker	Dracula
William Makepeace Thackeray	Vanity Fair
Oscar Wilde	The Picture of Dorian Gray

The Oxford World's Classics Website

www.worldsclassics.co.uk

- Browse the full range of Oxford World's Classics online
- Sign up for our monthly e-alert to receive information on new titles
- Read extracts from the Introductions
- Listen to our editors and translators talk about the world's greatest literature with our Oxford World's Classics audio guides
- Join the conversation, follow us on Twitter at OWC_Oxford
- Teachers and lecturers can order inspection copies quickly and simply via our website

www.worldsclassics.co.uk

MORE ABOUT **OXFORD WORLD'S CLASSICS**